SPILLING THE CAREER TEA

YOUR GUIDE TO
VALUE, INTENT, CREDIBILITY, AND CONFIDENCE

JERRY D. GOLDSTEIN
Edited by AnnaClare Sung
Photography by Jarret Birnbaum
Design by Jared Goldstein

"When asked for advice, give guidance. When asked for guidance, give coaching. When uncertain of what is being asked for, give opportunities and connections."

Spilling The Career Tea: Your Guide to Value, Intent, Credibility, & Confidence
A Practical Roadmap for College Students and Graduates Entering the Workforce
Show your value. Own your voice. Start your career with confidence.

Table of Contents

Introduction

The Dinner That Changed Everything

In the early 1980s, I attended a college fair at the Hartford Civic Center. There were no smartphones, no internet, and no digital college search tools. What I had was a 5.5 pound book called *Barron's Profiles of American Colleges,* a literal encyclopedia of higher education. College hopefuls flipped through it, circled schools, and requested brochures and applications either by phone or mail. That was the process.

My parents had one rule: I could apply anywhere in the country, as long as I had a close relative within an hour's drive in case of an emergency. So there I was, walking through rows of tables staffed by college reps, trying to make sense of the sea of options. I stopped at the University of Florida's table, flipped open my Barron's guide, and realized Gainesville wasn't an option since I had no family nearby. But then I saw *The University of Miami.* I knew where Miami was. I'd been there. I liked it.

I found the University of Miami table and met a professionally dressed, warm, and slightly weary woman named Mary. She greeted me with a smile and handed me a pen that read *1983 National Football Champions.* She asked me questions that made me think about who I was and who I wanted to become. We chatted for a while, and I noticed she seemed exhausted, yawning, excusing herself, clearly running on fumes. She was alone, far from home, and I sensed she could use a break.

So I did something unexpected. I invited her to dinner at my house.

She paused, surprised, and then said, "I would love that. Thank you so much."

I called my mom from a pay phone. She was home. I told her I'd invited someone from the University of Miami to dinner. Her name was Mary. That's all I knew. My mom said, "Okay, pick up a pie on your way home."

My dad came home early. My parents grilled me: What time is she coming? How is she getting here? What does she do at the university? Do you want to go there? I didn't know. All I knew was that she was kind, and she looked like she could use a good meal.

Mary Conway, Director of Admissions at the University of Miami, showed up for dinner. We talked, laughed, and connected. A week later, I received a handwritten thank you note, an application with the fee waived, and instructions to send it directly to her. Three weeks later, I was accepted.

That dinner changed my life; that brief conversation planted a seed. It was the first time I realized that career development wasn't just about choosing a major or landing a job, it was about discovering your voice, building confidence, and learning how to show up in the world with purpose.

Years later, that moment still guides me. I've had the privilege of coaching thousands of students and early career professionals, helping them navigate everything from resume writing and interview prep to emotional readiness and workplace dynamics. I took notes; lots of them. I tracked the questions, the patterns, the breakthroughs.

Spilling the Career Tea is the result of those years of listening, learning, and guiding. It's a practical, honest, and accessible resource for anyone preparing to enter the workforce or looking to grow in their early career. Whether you're a student wondering what employers are really looking for, or a new professional trying to find your footing, this guide offers a roadmap of competencies, from communication and critical thinking to digital presence and resilience, that will help you thrive.

This book isn't meant to be read once and shelved. It's a reference, a companion, and a confidence booster. My hope is that it gives you a head start, helps you ask better questions, and reminds you that you're not alone on this journey.

"Career readiness isn't about having all the answers; it's about building the mindset, skills, and confidence to keep asking the right questions."

Jerry D. Goldstein

The Skills I Didn't Know I Had

Looking back, I realize inviting Mary to dinner wasn't just about kindness, it was about instinctively demonstrating skills that would shape my personal and professional life:

- Empathy: I saw someone who needed support and offered it.
- Initiative: I took action without being prompted.
- Communication: I made a connection and followed through.
- Relationship building: I created trust and rapport in a short time.
- Adaptability: I navigated uncertainty with confidence.

These are the very skills employers look for today. They're not just "soft skills", they're *essential skills*. They attract mentors, colleagues, and friends. They helped me build a career, launch initiatives, and even meet my wife.

Why This Book Matters

That story is why I'm writing this book. Career readiness isn't just about resumes and interviews, it's about developing the mindset, habits, and skills that help you thrive in a competitive world. Whether you're a student entering the workforce or a professional starting out, the following chapters will guide you through what it takes to stand out, connect meaningfully, and build a career that reflects your values and strengths.

Let's begin.

Chapter 1: The VICC

This chapter introduces the VICC framework, Value, Intent & Credibility, and Confidence, as a transformative approach to job searching and career readiness. Readers will learn why traditional methods like polished resumes and LinkedIn profiles often fall short, and how VICC helps candidates stand out in a crowded application pool. Through Brittany's story, the chapter demonstrates how uncovering a unique value proposition, building authentic confidence, and applying intentional strategies create a compelling professional narrative. By the end of the chapter, readers will understand how to shift from passive applications to purposeful engagement, positioning themselves as credible, high impact professionals employers want to hire.

It was the spring of senior year, and Brittany was stuck.

She had the grades. She had the internships. She had the LinkedIn profile polished to perfection. But every time she hit "submit" on a job application, it felt like her resume disappeared into a black hole. No callbacks. No interviews. Just silence.

Brittany wasn't alone. Her classmates felt it too; the creeping anxiety that comes when you've done everything "right" but still feel invisible to employers. One night, after another rejection email, Brittany sat down with her mentor, a seasoned professional named

Michael who had built hiring pipelines for Fortune 500 companies.

Michael didn't ask for Brittany's resume. He asked her one question:

"What's your VICC?"

Brittany blinked. "My what?"

"Your VICC," Michael said. "Your **V**alue, your **I**ntent & **C**redibility, and your **C**onfidence. Employers don't hire resumes. They hire people who know what they bring to the table, believe in it, and show up with purpose."

That night, everything changed.

V: Unique Value Proposition

Michael helped Brittany uncover her unique value proposition; her skills *and* her story. She wasn't just a marketing major. She was a bilingual communicator who had grown up translating for her immigrant parents, giving her a natural ability to simplify complex ideas for diverse audiences. That was her edge.

Brittany rewrote her elevator pitch, her resume summary, and even her cover letters to reflect this value. Suddenly, her applications felt alive. They told a story. They had a heartbeat.

C: Confidence

Next came confidence. Brittany had always been humble, maybe too humble. She didn't want to sound arrogant, so she downplayed her achievements. Michael challenged her to own her wins.

"Confidence isn't arrogance," he said. "It's clarity. It's knowing your worth and communicating it without apology."

They practiced mock interviews. Brittany learned to speak about her experiences with conviction. She stopped saying "I helped with" and started saying "I led." She stopped shrinking and started showing up.

I: Intent & Credibility

Finally, Michael taught her the power of intent and credibility. Brittany began researching companies deeply before applying. She tailored her outreach to show she understood their mission and could contribute meaningfully. She followed up with thoughtful questions, shared relevant articles, and even connected with alumni working at her target firms.

Her applications weren't generic anymore; they were **intentional**. And her credibility grew with every interaction.

The Result

Within six weeks, Brittany had interviews at three top firms. Within eight, she had two offers. She chose the one that aligned most with her values, and she walked into her first day not just prepared but empowered.

Why VICC Matters

Brittany's story isn't unique because she got hired. It's unique because she learned to lead her job search with VICC. By aligning their story, skills, and strategy through VICC, candidates rise above generic applications and present themselves as intentional, credible professionals who add value to the workplace.

The chapters ahead position VICC as a framework that transforms how early career professionals present themselves to the world, and demonstrate how to apply it to your own journey. Whether you're a student, a recent grad, or someone pivoting into a new field, this book will help you build a career readiness system that employers recognize, respect, and reward.

Chapter 2: Why Career Competencies Matter

This chapter explores why employers prioritize career readiness beyond degrees, the shift in expectations driven by evolving industries and AI, and which competencies remain "AI-proof." It also provides practical strategies for students to build and track these skills through internships, leadership roles, certifications, and alumni engagement. Ultimately, career competencies transform knowledge into action, positioning graduates to lead, innovate, and thrive in an ever changing professional landscape.

A college degree may open doors, but it no longer guarantees career success on its own. Employers today seek professionals who can apply knowledge in dynamic, real world environments, communicating effectively, collaborating across diverse teams, solving complex problems, and adapting to rapid change. Career competencies bridge the gap between academic learning and workplace performance, reducing onboarding time and increasing productivity. These skills, such as critical thinking, professionalism, technology fluency, and equity & inclusion, signal versatility, resilience, and a growth mindset, qualities that make graduates valuable contributors from day one.

Why Employers Value Career Readiness Beyond Degrees

Competencies do not replace education.—there is no substitute for the degree. However, skill development is essential as a supplement to the college experience. Employers prioritize career readiness because it bridges the gap between academic knowledge and workplace performance. A degree demonstrates subject expertise, but it doesn't guarantee the ability to communicate effectively, collaborate in diverse teams, or adapt to fast changing environments. Career competencies, such as critical thinking, professionalism, and technology fluency, equip candidates to handle real world challenges from day one, reducing onboarding time and increasing productivity. In short, career readiness signals that a candidate can apply what they know in practical, high pressure situations, making them a lower risk and higher value hire.

The Shift in Employer Expectations

In the past, a candidate's degree indicated their career capability. However, today's competitive job market and rapidly evolving industries require professionals who think critically, collaborate effectively, and navigate real-world challenges. Employers recognize that a degree alone does not guarantee the ability to:

- Communicate professionally in workplace settings.
- Work efficiently in teams or manage workplace relationships.
- Problem-solve under pressure.

- Adapt to new technologies and industry changes.

Career readiness ensures that employees can transition smoothly from academia to professional environments, reducing the need for extensive training while increasing efficiency and productivity.

Key Career Competencies Employers Value
Employers prioritize candidates who demonstrate essential career competencies beyond technical knowledge. These include:

- Communication Skills: Articulating thoughts clearly in emails, meetings, and presentations.
- Teamwork and Collaboration: Working well with others across departments and backgrounds.
- Critical Thinking and Problem Solving: Making informed decisions under complex circumstances.
- Professionalism and Work Ethic: Reliability, accountability, and ethical behavior in workplace settings.
- Technology Skills: Understanding and utilizing digital tools relevant to the industry.
- Equity & Inclusion: Being aware and contributing to diverse and inclusive work environments.
- Leadership & Initiative: Taking ownership of responsibilities and inspiring others.
- Career & Self Development: Actively pursuing growth through feedback, learning

opportunities, and professional development to
stay competitive

These competencies make candidates versatile,
resourceful, and ready to contribute effectively from
day one.

The Importance of Adaptability
Modern workplaces are dynamic, requiring employees
who can adjust to change, learn quickly, and embrace
innovation. Degrees provide foundational knowledge,
but career readiness ensures professionals can thrive as
industries evolve.

For example, in fields like technology, marketing, and
healthcare, trends shift rapidly. Professionals must
continuously develop their skill sets to stay competitive.
Employers favor individuals who display a growth
mindset, proactively seek new learning opportunities,
and demonstrate resilience in the face of change.

Imagine if you were one of the first people to master
Microsoft Windows? In 1985, a new interface was
released to simplify user interaction. It revolutionized
the way we worked. Windows is now discontinued, yet
we all know what it was. Do we know what's next?

How Students Can Build Career Readiness
Students and graduates can practice career readiness by
engaging in:

> ➡ Internships and Work Experience - Gaining
> hands-on exposure to professional environments.

➡ Networking and Mentorships - Learning from experienced professionals and making industry connections.

➡ Extracurricular Leadership Roles - Demonstrating teamwork, initiative, and problem-solving skills.

➡ Workshops and Certifications - Expanding practical knowledge beyond traditional coursework.

➡ Alumni Engagement Activities - Mentoring, Site Visits, Job Shadowing, Networking, and more.

Employers appreciate candidates who show initiative in preparing for their careers, rather than solely relying on their degrees.

How Students Can Track Career Readiness

Offering a co-curricular transcript is quite innovative and relatively unique, especially when integrated with experiential learning tracking. While some institutions have begun exploring this concept, few have implemented it in a way that's deeply embedded in mentoring, career development, and alumni engagement like software companies such as PeopleGrove are poised to do.

Not every student has access to a formal co-curricular transcript, but career readiness can still be tracked through intentional self-documentation. Start by creating a simple competency log or spreadsheet where you record experiences, such as internships, leadership roles, and projects, and link them to key skills like communication, teamwork, and problem solving. Digital portfolios and LinkedIn profiles are excellent tools for showcasing these experiences publicly. Students can also use career readiness frameworks, such as NACE's eight competencies, as a checklist to self-assess progress. Keeping track of certifications, micro-credentials, and feedback from mentors provides tangible evidence of growth. By actively documenting and reflecting on these activities, students build a clear narrative of their professional development, even without an official transcript.

How AI Is Changing Employer Expectations
Artificial intelligence is transforming the workplace, and with it, the expectations employers have for new hires. While AI automates routine tasks and analyzes vast amounts of data, it doesn't replace the uniquely human skills driving innovation, collaboration, and ethical decision making.

Employers are now looking for professionals who can:

- Interpret and apply AI-generated insights in real world contexts.
- Collaborate effectively in human/AI teams.
- Demonstrate ethical awareness in the use of data and technology.
- Embrace continuous learning to stay ahead of emerging tools and trends.

AI is not replacing career competencies, it's redefining which ones matter most.

Which Competencies Become MORE Valuable with AI
Rather than making career competencies obsolete, AI increases the value of certain skills. These include:

- Critical Thinking and Problem Solving: Evaluating AI outputs, identifying limitations, and making sound decisions.
- Communication Skills: Translating complex data into clear, actionable insights for diverse audiences.
- Equity & Inclusion: Ensuring AI systems are used in ways that promote fairness and reduce bias.
- Career & Self Development: Staying current with technological trends and pursuing relevant credentials.
- Leadership & Initiative: Guiding teams through digital transformation and championing responsible innovation.

These competencies help professionals not just survive but thrive in an AI augmented workplace.

Skills That Are "AI Proof"
Some skills remain uniquely human and are unlikely to be automated. These "AI proof" competencies include:

- Empathy and Emotional Intelligence - Understanding people, building trust, and navigating complex relationships.
- Ethical Judgment - Making values-based decisions in ambiguous or high stakes situations.

- Creativity and Innovation - Generating original ideas, storytelling, and designing novel solutions.
- Mentorship and Coaching - Supporting others' growth through lived experience and personal connection.

These skills are essential for leadership, community-building, and long-term career success.

How Students Can Prepare for an AI Augmented Future
Students can build AI fluency and future proof their careers by:

➥ Completing foundational AI credentials (e.g., Salesforce's "AgentBlazer" and IBM's "Getting Started with AI").

➥ Participating in interdisciplinary projects that combine technology with human-centered problem solving.

➥ Engaging in mentorship and alumni networks to learn how professionals are adapting to AI.

➥ Reflecting on the ethical and social impacts of AI in coursework and co-curricular activities.

AI is not the end of human work, it's a new beginning. The professionals who succeed will be those who combine technical fluency with timeless human competencies.

Final Flex

A diploma may open doors, but career readiness ensures long term success. Employers seek well rounded professionals who can communicate, collaborate, think critically, and adapt to change. By developing career competencies, students and graduates enhance their employability, positioning themselves as valuable contributors in the workforce. Ultimately, degrees provide knowledge, but career readiness transforms knowledge into action, making it an essential factor in professional success. Students can start building relationships and connections with what is likely to be their most valuable network, their alumni base.

Chapter 3: Emotional Readiness to Enter the Workforce & Resiliency

This chapter focuses on the emotional readiness and resilience required for new graduates and early career professionals transitioning into the workforce. It explores the challenges of adapting to workplace expectations, managing stress, and overcoming setbacks. Special attention is given to Gen Z, who face unique pressures such as remote work isolation, social media driven career FOMO, and balancing side hustles with traditional career paths. The chapter emphasizes strategies for maintaining mental health, negotiating flexibility, and building resilience when ideal conditions aren't available. Practical tips include clarifying priorities, mastering time management, seeking mentorship, and reframing rejection as a learning opportunity. Ultimately, success is framed as the ability to learn, adapt, and grow through challenges rather than avoiding them.

Transitioning from college to the workforce is a huge shift. New graduates must adapt to new responsibilities, face setbacks, and learn how to cope with stress. Emotional resilience is key to overcoming obstacles and thriving in a professional environment.

Thriving in the Workplace: Managing Expectations, Handling Stress, and Staying Resilient
Entering the workforce as a new college graduate or early career professional is both exciting and overwhelming. The transition from school to a full-time job brings new challenges, expectations, and pressures that can sometimes feel difficult to navigate—whether it's adapting to a workplace setting, facing rejection, or maintaining motivation. Learning how to manage stress, build resilience, and prioritize self-care is essential for long-term success and personal well-being, especially when facing these challenges.

Gen Z - Specific Challenges in the Workplace
Gen Z professionals bring fresh perspectives, digital fluency, and a strong sense of purpose to the workforce. However, they also face unique emotional and cultural challenges that can impact their career readiness and resilience.

1. Remote Work Anxiety and Isolation

While remote work offers flexibility, it can also lead to feelings of disconnection, loneliness, and uncertainty. Without in-person interactions, Gen Z employees may struggle to build relationships, initiate mentorship, or feel part of a team. Unlike older generations, many Gen Z professionals began their careers during or after the pandemic, meaning remote work was often their first professional experience. They didn't have the benefit of building foundational workplace habits, like networking, mentorship, and team collaboration, in an in person environment before transitioning to remote work.

2. Social Media Comparison and Career FOMO
Constant exposure to curated success stories on LinkedIn, Instagram, and TikTok can create unrealistic expectations and feelings of inadequacy. Career FOMO (Fear of Missing Out) can lead to anxiety, self-doubt, and pressure to "keep up" with peers.

3. Side Hustle vs. Traditional Career Paths
Gen Z often explores multiple income streams, creative projects, and entrepreneurial ventures. While this can be empowering, it may also create tension with traditional career structures and expectations around loyalty, focus, and long term planning.

To balance multiple income streams with traditional career expectations, Gen Z professionals can adopt strategies that foster trust and long term growth. Transparent communication with employers about side projects helps prevent misunderstandings, while strong time management ensures primary job responsibilities remain a priority. Aligning side hustles with career goals can turn entrepreneurial ventures into skill building opportunities, and seeking mentorship from professionals experienced in portfolio careers provides guidance on navigating loyalty and planning. Employers can also play a role by offering flexible policies and recognizing that multi-stream careers are becoming the norm, creating a culture that values both creativity and commitment.

Work Life Balance
Gen Z values mental health, flexibility, and purpose driven work. They may push back against outdated norms like hustle culture or rigid schedules, advocating instead for balance, boundaries, and meaningful engagement.

Gen Z's emphasis on mental health, flexibility, and purpose driven work influences career readiness by reshaping expectations of professional life. Rather than prioritizing long hours or rigid schedules, they seek roles that support well-being and meaningful impact, which can lead to tension in traditional work environments. Career readiness for this generation involves learning how to advocate for balance while meeting organizational goals, negotiating flexibility without compromising reliability, and building resilience when ideal conditions aren't immediately available. These skills ensure Gen Z can thrive while staying true to their values.

- **Clarify Priorities:** Identify what balance and purpose mean to you and communicate these values during interviews and performance reviews.
- **Learn Negotiation Skills:** Practice negotiating flexibility (remote work, hybrid schedules) while demonstrating reliability and productivity.

- **Develop Resilience:** Prepare for situations where ideal conditions aren't available by reframing challenges as growth opportunities.
- **Master Time Management:** Use tools like time blocking and task prioritization to maintain boundaries without sacrificing performance.
- **Seek Mentorship:** Connect with professionals who successfully integrate well being and purpose into their careers for guidance and perspective.
- **Build Emotional Intelligence:** Strengthen skills in empathy, adaptability, and stress management to thrive in diverse work environments.
- **Stay Goal-Oriented:** Set clear short term and long term goals to maintain motivation even when conditions aren't perfect.

While advocating for balance is important, it's worth remembering that your first job(s) may not offer perfect work life harmony. Sometimes you need to pay your dues and demonstrate your value before earning greater flexibility and autonomy.

Managing Expectations and Handling Workplace Stress

One of the biggest adjustments for new professionals is learning that workplaces operate differently than classrooms. In school, assignments come with clear instructions, deadlines, and grading systems, while at work, projects can be ambiguous, feedback may be inconsistent, and success is often measured by broader contributions.

Common Workplace Challenges:

- Workload Pressures: Deadlines, multitasking, and balancing responsibilities.
- Learning Curve: Adapting to professional tools, communication styles, and workflows.
- Feedback & Growth: Heeding and responding to constructive criticism.

Strategies for Managing Expectations and Stress:

1. Understand Your Role and Goals - Clarify responsibilities and performance expectations with your manager.
2. Ask Questions and Seek Support - Don't hesitate to ask for guidance from colleagues and mentors.
3. Set Realistic Goals - Break down tasks into manageable steps to avoid feeling overwhelmed.
4. Recognize That Perfection Isn't Required - Growth comes from trial and error; mistakes are learning opportunities.
5. Practice Stress Management Techniques - Deep breathing, taking breaks, and organizing tasks can reduce anxiety.

Overcoming Rejection and Learning from Failures
No one enjoys rejection or failure, but both are inevitable parts of professional growth. Whether it's not landing a dream job, receiving critical feedback, or

making mistakes at work, setbacks should be seen as learning experiences rather than personal shortcomings.

How to Reframe Rejection and Failure:

1. View Criticism as a Tool for Improvement- Employers want to see you succeed; feedback helps refine your skills.
2. Recognize Growth in Every Experience- Failures teach lessons that contribute to long term success.
3. Stay Objective, Not Emotional-   Separate personal identity from work results to maintain confidence.
4. Adapt and Move Forward- Use each setback to refine strategies and approach challenges with newfound wisdom.

Famous Failure to Success Stories:

- Oprah Winfrey was fired from her first TV job and told she was "unfit for television."
- Steve Jobs was ousted from Apple before returning to lead its most successful era.
- J.K. Rowling faced multiple rejections before publishing Harry Potter.
  These stories remind us that failure is not the opposite of success, it's often the path to it.

The "Failure Résumé" Exercise:
Create a résumé that lists your biggest setbacks: jobs you didn't get, projects that flopped, ideas that didn't land. For each, write what you learned and how it shaped your growth. This exercise builds self-awareness, humility, and resilience.

Reframing Rejection as Market Research:
Every rejection is data. It tells you something about the market, your positioning, or your approach. Instead of internalizing rejection, analyze it. What can you adjust? What patterns are emerging? What feedback keeps showing up? Talk to people about your rejection and get feedback from others.

Practicing Self Care While Maintaining Motivation
Balancing professional responsibilities with personal well-being is critical for long term career success. Burnout and exhaustion can negatively impact productivity, creativity, and overall job satisfaction, making self-care a priority.

Ways to Maintain Motivation and Well Being:
1. Prioritize Work Life Balance: Avoid overworking, schedule downtime and relaxation.
2. Celebrate Small Wins: Acknowledge progress and accomplishments to stay motivated.
3. Stay Connected with Support Systems: Mentors, friends, and colleagues provide encouragement and perspective.
4. Engage in Activities That Recharge You: Exercise, hobbies, and mindfulness reduce stress.
5. Set Personal and Professional Goals: Clear objectives provide direction and excitement for the future.

Final Flex

Navigating the workforce as an early career professional comes with challenges, but learning to manage expectations, overcome setbacks, and prioritize self-care makes the journey much smoother. Gen Z professionals face unique pressures from remote work isolation to social media comparison but with emotional readiness and resilience, they can thrive. Success isn't about avoiding obstacles. It's about learning, adapting, and growing through them.

Chapter 4: Communication: The Key to Professional Success

Communication is more than exchanging words, it's the foundation of professional success. This chapter equips you with strategies to communicate effectively across verbal, written, nonverbal, and digital channels. You'll learn how to craft clear messages, listen actively, and ask insightful questions that build trust and open doors. From video call etiquette and social media presence to reframing statements for impact and resolving workplace conflicts, these skills help you stand out in interviews, thrive in team settings, and strengthen your personal brand. By mastering communication, you position yourself as a confident, collaborative professional ready to deliver results and grow your career.

Effective communication is at the heart of professional success. Whether you're interacting with colleagues, clients, or supervisors, strong communication skills foster collaboration, prevent misunderstandings, and enhance productivity. Effective communication relies as much on a message's delivery, interpretation, and response, as it does on the message's content. Mastering verbal, written, and nonverbal communication, practicing active listening, and navigating workplace conflicts with effective dialogue are essential for career growth and maintaining healthy professional relationships.

Verbal, Written, and Nonverbal Communication Strategies

Effective communication comes in many forms, each playing a critical role in professional interactions. A well-articulated message can boost teamwork, leadership, and workplace efficiency.

1. Verbal Communication: Speaking Clearly and Persuasively

Verbal communication is central to meetings, presentations, and daily conversations. Professionals must express ideas with clarity, confidence, and purpose.

Example:

> During a quarterly strategy meeting at MacTech University, *Maria Chen,* a senior marketing strategist, proposes a new alumni engagement campaign called "RamConnect Reimagined." She aims to increase alumni participation in mentoring programs by 40% over the next academic year.
>
> To make her case, Maria uses a structured outline that begins with a compelling data point: a recent survey showing that 72% of alumni are interested in giving back through mentorship, but don't know how to get involved. She then highlights the campaign's key benefits, streamlined onboarding, personalized outreach, and jumpstarts integration with existing software platforms like PeopleGrove.

Maria modulates her tone to match the room: confident and energetic when discussing projected outcomes, and calm and deliberate when addressing budget concerns. Her concise delivery and persuasive framing help leadership see the campaign's viability, ultimately securing approval and funding for a fall launch.

Best Practices:

- Organize your thoughts before speaking.
- Use a confident and engaging tone.
- Adapt speech to the audience, i.e. formal for executives, more relaxed with teammates.
- Avoid jargon when explaining complex concepts.

2. Written Communication: Conveying Messages with Precision

Written communication is just as critical as verbal interactions. Emails, reports, and project documentation must be clear, structured, and professional to ensure recipients understand the message correctly.

Example:

At MacTech University, *Daniel Rivera*, a project manager overseeing the rollout of a new alumni engagement platform, needs to inform stakeholders about a two week deadline extension due to unexpected integration issues with the university's legacy systems.

Instead of sending a vague update, Daniel drafts a clear and proactive email:

Subject: Updated Launch Timeline for Alumni Platform

Dear Team,

I wanted to inform you that the launch date for the alumni engagement platform has been moved from September 15 to September 29. This extension is necessary to address compatibility issues identified during final testing with our legacy systems.

To minimize disruption, we're implementing a phased rollout and increasing support resources during the transition. I'll share a revised timeline and updated onboarding materials by end of day tomorrow.

Please let me know if you have any questions or concerns.

Best,
Daniel

Via concise, informative, and solution oriented language, Daniel maintains trust and keeps the project on track.

Instead of writing a vague email, he:

1. Clearly states the new deadline.
2. Provides a reason for the delay.

3. Offers solutions to mitigate the impact.

Best Practices:

- Keep messages direct and professional.
- Use bullet points for easy readability.
- Double-check grammar and clarity before sending important emails.
- Tailor tone based on audience, i.e. formal for leadership, conversational for coworkers.

3. Nonverbal Communication: Reinforcing Messages Without Words

Nonverbal cues influence how spoken and written messages are perceived. Body language, facial expressions, and tone contribute to credibility, engagement, and trust building in professional interactions.

Example:

> During an interview for a marketing coordinator role at a nonprofit organization, *Aisha Patel* walks into the room with a calm, confident demeanor. She maintains steady eye contact with each panelist, sits upright with relaxed shoulders, and uses open hand gestures while discussing her experience managing social media campaigns.
>
> Her body language reinforces her verbal responses, making her appear engaged, self-assured, and well prepared. In contrast, another candidate earlier in the day had slouched in their chair, avoided eye contact, and kept their arms

crossed leaving the panel uncertain about their enthusiasm and confidence.

Aisha's nonverbal communication plays a key role in how the interviewers perceive her competence and professionalism, ultimately helping her stand out as a top candidate.

Best Practices:
- Maintain good posture to show confidence.
- Use eye contact to demonstrate attentiveness.
- Avoid crossed arms, which may signal defensiveness.
- Smile and nod to encourage open communication.

Mastering verbal, written, and nonverbal communication ensures messages are effectively conveyed, understood, and well received in professional settings.

Active Listening and Asking the Right Questions
Communication isn't just about speaking well, it's also about listening effectively.

1. The Power of Active Listening
Active listening involves fully concentrating, understanding, and responding thoughtfully rather than simply hearing words. It fosters collaboration and ensures workplace conversations are productive.

Example:

> *Jordan Carlson*, a junior communications associate at MacTech University, feels overwhelmed by a tight deadline for an upcoming alumni newsletter. He schedules a quick check-in with his manager, *Tanya Brooks*, to discuss the challenge.
>
> During the meeting, Tanya maintains eye contact, nods as Jordan explains the issue, and listens without interrupting. Instead of brushing off his concerns, she acknowledges the pressure and offers a practical solution: reallocating one of the stories to a later issue and looping in a senior writer to help with editing.
>
> Jordan leaves the conversation feeling heard and supported. Tanya's attentive body language and constructive response not only ease his stress but also reinforce a culture of trust and collaboration within the team.

Best Practices:

- Listen without interrupting and reflect before responding.
- Summarize the speaker's points to ensure understanding.
- Use phrases like, "To clarify, what you're saying is…" to confirm details.
- Pay attention to the tone and emotions behind words.

2. Asking the Right Questions to Strengthen Conversations

Well-crafted questions drive meaningful dialogue, encourage deeper insights, and foster better decision making.

Example:

> During a brainstorming session at MacTech University's Office of Alumni Relations, *Rachel Kim*, the associate director, gathers her team to develop fresh ideas for increasing alumni engagement through RamConnect.
>
> Instead of opening with a broad question like "What should we do?" Rachel frames the discussion strategically:
>
> "How can we deepen alumni involvement in mentoring and career development?"
>
> This phrasing helps guide Rachel's team, toward creative, mission-driven ideas. The conversation quickly moves from generic suggestions to targeted proposals, such as integrating alumni spotlights into RamConnect and launching themed networking weeks tied to industry sectors.
>
> Rachel's intentional framing fosters strategic thinking and ensures the brainstorming session yields actionable, aligned outcomes.

You don't need to be a team leader like Rachel to benefit from asking the right questions. For students and recent graduates, thoughtful questions can transform networking conversations, interviews, and mentorship sessions into powerful career building opportunities.

Employers and mentors notice curiosity and preparation. Strategic questions show that you're engaged, eager to learn, and focused on growth; qualities that stand out in competitive job markets.

Frame your questions around impact and growth, not just your needs. This approach signals professionalism and helps you uncover actionable advice that accelerates your career journey.

Best Practices:

- Ask open ended questions to invite discussion.
- Seek clarification when details are unclear.
- Use questions to spark problem solving and creativity.
- Avoid leading questions that bias responses.

By listening actively and asking insightful questions, professionals strengthen workplace relationships and enhance collaboration.

Digital Communication: Navigating the Modern Workplace
In today's hybrid and tech driven work environments, digital communication is no longer optional, it's foundational. How professionals present themselves online shapes their credibility, visibility, and career trajectory.

Gen Z professionals are entering the workforce with digital fluency but must learn to apply it strategically in professional settings. Digital communication is not just about being online, it's about being intentional, respectful, and authentic.

Video Call Presence and Virtual Meeting Skills
Remote and hybrid work have made video calls a daily reality. Your presence on screen matters just as much as your presence in the room.

Example:

> During a virtual team huddle on Microsoft Teams, *Brianna Cloud,* a Gen Z UX designer, shares her screen to walk through a prototype. She uses concise language, pauses for feedback, and monitors the chat for questions. Her professional setup and confident delivery earn praise from her manager and help move the project forward.

Best Practices:
- Position your camera at eye level with good lighting and a clean background.
- Even in remote settings, attire influences perception.
- Nod, smile, and use hand gestures to show attentiveness.
- Stay muted when not speaking but avoid being passive.

- Contribute insights or links without derailing the conversation.

Social Media Professional Presence
Social media is a powerful tool for career development, but it requires intentionality. Gen Z professionals often blend personal and professional identities online, which can be an asset if managed well.

Example:

> *Jalen Smith*, a recent graduate, creates TikTok videos about his job search journey, resume tips, and interview experiences. One video goes viral, leading to a feature in a career blog and a direct message from a recruiter. His authentic content builds visibility and opens doors.

Best Practices:

- LinkedIn - Share insights, celebrate milestones, and engage with industry content.
- TikTok - Use short form video to showcase skills, share career tips, or document your journey.
- Instagram - Highlight creative work, community involvement, or personal branding.
- Privacy Settings - Be mindful of what's public and what's personal.

Text, Slack, and Teams Communication Etiquette
Instant messaging platforms like Slack and Teams are central to workplace communication. Tone, timing, and clarity matter more than ever.

Example:

> Instead of emailing, *Maya Thompson* pings her supervisor on Slack:
>
> > "Hi @Alex, quick update: the alumni dashboard mockup is ready for review. Link: [Figma]. Let me know if you'd like to meet to walk through it."
>
> Her message is direct, respectful, and action-oriented, ideal for fast paced environments.

Best Practices:
- Be Clear and Concise - Avoid long blocks of text; use bullet points or threads.
- Respect Boundaries - Don't expect instant replies; use status indicators.
- Use Emojis Sparingly - They can add warmth but may be misinterpreted.
- Tag Thoughtfully - Use @mentions to direct attention, not to overwhelm.
- Avoid Overuse of "Hey" or "Quick Question" - Get to the point respectfully.

Personal Branding Through Communication
Every message you send, whether verbal, written, or digital, contributes to your personal brand. Gen Z

professionals often build their brand across platforms, blending authenticity with professionalism.

Influencer Style Example:

> *Taylor Morgan*, a Gen Z career coach, uses LinkedIn to post weekly "Career Tea" threads, short, engaging posts with tips, humor, and real talk. Her posts consistently get thousands of views, leading to speaking invitations and brand partnerships.

Best Practices:

- Consistency Across Channels - Align your tone, values, and visuals.
- Share Your Voice - Use storytelling to highlight your journey, values, and goals.
- Engage Thoughtfully - Comment, repost, and contribute to conversations in your field.
- Build a Portfolio - Use platforms like LinkedIn, Instagram, or TikTok to showcase work.

Reframing Statements: Making Your Message About Them

In cover letters, interviews, and professional conversations, it's natural to talk about yourself after all, you're selling your best self and your unique skills. But, especially when trying to make a strong first impression, too much "I" can come off as self-centered rather than solution oriented.

Why "I" Overuse Happens:
- It mirrors how we speak in everyday conversation.
- It feels natural when describing personal experiences.
- It's often encouraged in early writing instruction ("Tell your story!").

Shift your focus to the employer's needs, goals, and challenges. You want them to receive your message and think "We should talk to this person, they might make our lives easier." When writing a cover letter, instead of starting every paragraph with "I", try leading with the value you bring or the problem you solve. In interviews, frame your responses around impact and collaboration.

Why This Matters:
Employers are looking for people who solve problems, add value, and make their lives easier. who solve problems, add value, and make their work easier. Your goal is to persuade them that you can deliver those outcomes. Direct your intention toward demonstrating impact; how your skills and actions create measurable results. Communicate your value by aligning your experience with their needs and priorities. Highlight results you've achieved, relevance to the role, and readiness to contribute immediately.

Instead of:
"I led a team of five interns to develop a new alumni outreach strategy."

Try:
"Led a team of five interns to develop an alumni outreach strategy that increased engagement by 30%."

Instead of:
"I'm passionate about helping students navigate career transitions."

Try:
"Bringing clarity and confidence to students navigating career transitions through mentorship, workshops."

Instead of:
"I created a content calendar for the university's social media channels."

Try:
"Developed a content calendar that aligned with university branding and increased social media engagement"

Instead of:
I am excited to apply for the marketing coordinator role. I believe my experience in social media and event planning…

Try:
Helping organizations grow through strategic social media and event planning is where my experience can be most valuable…

Instead of:
I managed the budget for our student organization.

Try:
Managed the budget to ensure responsible spending and maximize event impact for our student organization.

Navigating Workplace Conflicts with Effective Communication
Conflicts are inevitable in professional environments, but how they're addressed determines workplace harmony and productivity. Resolving misunderstandings requires empathy, strategic dialogue, and a solutions-focused approach.

1. Identifying the Root Cause of Conflict

Before resolving a dispute, it's important to understand why it happened. Miscommunication, differing expectations, or conflicting work styles often contribute to tensions.

Example:

> At MacTech University's Career Center, *Nipsey Russell* and *Everett Brown*, two team members working on the fall alumni networking event, begin to clash over task delegation. Both Nipsey

and Everett believe they're responsible for coordinating outreach to alumni speakers—Everett has already begun drafting emails.

The confusion stems from a vague project kickoff email that didn't clearly outline individual responsibilities. Tension rises during a planning meeting, but their supervisor, *Jasmine Ortiz*, steps in to mediate.

Jasmine calmly clarifies the roles: Nipsey will lead speaker outreach, while Everett will focus on event logistics and registration. She also updates the project tracker to reflect these assignments and encourages both team members to check in weekly to avoid future overlap.

By addressing the misunderstanding directly and reinforcing expectations, Jasmine prevents further disagreement and helps the team focus on their shared goals.

2. Conflict Resolution Through Clear and Calm Communication

Handling workplace disputes requires staying composed, listening to concerns, and proposing solutions professionally.

Example:

While reviewing the final draft of a donor impact report at MacTech University, *Don Rickles*, a senior communications officer, shares some critical feedback with *Lena Morales*, a junior team member who led the project.

Don points out that the messaging feels too generic and suggests that the alumni stories could be more emotionally compelling. Initially taken aback, Lena resists the urge to defend her work and instead responds constructively:

"I appreciate your feedback, Don. Can you specify which sections you think need stronger storytelling? I'd love to collaborate on refining those parts to better connect with our audience."

By acknowledging Don's perspective, seeking clarification, and offering to improve the work together, Lena turns a potentially tense moment into a productive exchange, strengthening both the project and their working relationship.

Instead of playing defense, Lena:

1. Acknowledged Don's perspective (e.g., "I appreciate your feedback.").
2. Clarified his concerns (e.g., "Can you specify which areas need improvement?").
   Offered solutions (e.g., "I'd love to collaborate on refining these aspects.").

Best Practices:

- Stay neutral and avoid personal attacks.
- Focus on solutions, not blame.
- Acknowledge different perspectives without dismissing them.

- Use "I" statements instead of accusatory language (e.g., "I think we should…" instead of "You're wrong.").

Effective communication helps resolve conflicts professionally and diplomatically, maintaining positive workplace relationships.

3. Understand what is being asked of you.

Understanding communication preferences and following instructions precisely is essential. Proactively clarifying your supervisor's expectations and adapting your communication style to the situation builds trust and effectiveness in professional relationships.

Example:

> *Geraldine Jones*, a new associate in MacTech University's Advancement Office, is asked by her supervisor, *Charles Wilson*, to call a long time donor and find out when they'd like to meet to discuss a new scholarship initiative.
>
> Geraldine, who feels more comfortable with written communication, decides to send an email instead of making the call. Two days later, Charles checks in and asks, "Did you call the donor?" Geraldine replies, "Yes, I reached out," assuming her email counts as fulfilling the request.
>
> However Charles knows the donor well and reminds Geraldine that the donor specifically prefers phone calls and rarely checks email. The

meeting hasn't been scheduled, and the donor may now feel overlooked.

This moment becomes a learning opportunity for Geraldine. Charles explains that communication isn't just about delivering a message, it's about choosing the right method for the audience. Geraldine realizes that while email felt easier, it didn't meet the expectations of either her supervisor or the donor.

Final Flex
Communication isn't just a workplace skill, it's the foundation of professional success. Whether verbal, written, or nonverbal, the way young professionals deliver messages impacts their collaboration, productivity, and leadership effectiveness. Active listening and asking thoughtful questions strengthen interactions and build trust, while conflict resolution through strategic communication ensures healthy work environments.

By mastering these communication techniques, professionals enhance their credibility, excel in teamwork, and foster long term career success.

Chapter 5: Teamwork: Thriving in Collaborative Environments

Teamwork is more than working side by side, it's about building trust, communicating clearly, and embracing diversity in today's fast paced, tech driven workplace. This chapter explores how collaboration fuels innovation and productivity, whether in traditional offices or virtual environments. You'll learn strategies for leading effective remote meetings, fostering relationships across time zones and cultures, and mastering digital tools that keep teams connected. We'll dive into the foundations of strong teamwork: trust, communication, shared goals, and show how to navigate different work styles and personalities. We'll tackle conflict resolution with practical tips for turning disagreements into opportunities for growth. By the end of this chapter, you'll understand how to thrive in collaborative environments and contribute to teams that deliver exceptional results.

No matter the industry, teamwork is essential. Employers expect professionals to work effectively with diverse groups of people. Understanding different perspectives and collaborating toward a common goal makes individuals valuable assets in any workplace.

The Power of Teamwork in the Workplace
Teamwork is the backbone of any successful organization. In today's workplace, no individual can thrive in isolation. Collaboration fosters innovation,

enhances productivity, and strengthens workplace culture. Employers value teamwork because it leads to stronger problem solving, efficiency, and creativity, making it a fundamental skill for professionals across all industries. Whether working on major projects or tackling everyday tasks, understanding the foundations of teamwork, learning how to manage different work styles and personalities, and effectively handling conflicts can help employees thrive in group environments.

Remote and Virtual Team Collaboration
In today's global and hybrid work environments, teamwork often happens across screens, time zones, and cultures. Virtual collaboration requires intentionality, empathy, and digital fluency. Whether leading a Zoom meeting, managing a Slack channel, or coordinating with international colleagues, professionals must adapt their teamwork strategies to thrive in remote settings.

Leading Virtual Meetings
Running a successful virtual meeting takes more than sending a calendar invite. It requires structure, engagement, and clarity.

Best Practices:
- Set Clear Objectives - Share an agenda in advance and define outcomes.

- Facilitate Participation - Use breakout rooms, polls, or chat prompts to involve everyone.
- Respect Time Zones - Schedule meetings that accommodate global team members.
  Follow Up - Summarize decisions and next steps in writing after the meeting.

Example:

At MacTech University, the RamConnect development team holds weekly Zoom standups. The team lead, Priya, starts each meeting with a quick round of updates, then opens the floor for blockers and feedback. She uses a shared Google Doc to track progress and assigns action items in real time. Her structured approach keeps the team aligned and productive even when half the members are remote.

Building Relationships Without Face to Face Interaction

Remote work can feel isolating, especially for early career professionals. Building trust and camaraderie takes effort when hallway chats and coffee breaks are not an option.

Example:

Tariq O'Connor, a new hire at a MacTech University global edtech firm, joins a remote team spread across five countries. To build relationships, he initiates short "get to know you" calls with each teammate and creates a

shared playlist for the team's weekly wrap ups.
His efforts help foster a sense of belonging and
collaboration, even across borders.

Strategies:

1. Schedule Virtual 1:1s - Regular check-ins foster
    connection and mentorship.
2. Use Informal Channels - Slack "watercooler"
    threads or virtual coffee chats help build
    rapport.
3. Celebrate Wins - Acknowledge achievements
    publicly to boost morale.
4. Be Present - Respond promptly, show
    appreciation, and engage authentically.

Managing Across Time Zones and Cultures
Global teams bring diverse perspectives, but also
logistical challenges. Successful collaboration requires
cultural sensitivity and time zone awareness.

Example:

> *Sylvia Franklin*, a project manager at a
> nonprofit, oversees a team with members in
> New York, Nairobi, and Sydney. She rotates
> meeting times monthly, uses Slack for
> asynchronous updates, and includes cultural
> notes in her onboarding materials. Her inclusive
> approach builds trust and keeps the team
> aligned.

Tips:

➡ Use Shared Calendars - Tools like Outlook's time zone view help coordinate meetings.

➡ Rotate Meeting Times - Share the burden of early or late calls.

➡ Be Culturally Aware - Understand holidays, communication styles, and work norms.

➡ Document Decisions - Written records ensure clarity across asynchronous teams.

Mastering Digital Collaboration Tools
Digital tools are the backbone of remote teamwork. Mastery of platforms like Slack, Microsoft Teams, Google Workspace, Notion, and Trello can dramatically improve efficiency and communication.

Example:

> *Lila Dickens,* a communications coordinator, uses Notion to manage her team's editorial calendar. She integrates Slack notifications, embeds Google Docs, and tags teammates for approvals. Her digital fluency helps the team stay organized and meet deadlines with ease.

Best Practices:

- Choose the Right Tool for the Task - Use Slack for quick updates, Google Docs for collaboration, and Trello for task tracking.
- Organize Channels and Threads - Keep communication streamlined and searchable.

- Set Norms - Define expectations for response times, tagging, and file sharing.
- Stay Updated - Learn new features and shortcuts to maximize productivity.

The Foundations of Successful Teamwork
A high performing team doesn't just happen; it is built on essential principles that drive collaboration and effectiveness. Successful teamwork requires trust, clear communication, shared goals, and accountability.

1. Establishing Trust and Mutual Respect

Trust is the cornerstone of teamwork. When colleagues trust one another, they collaborate more openly, share ideas freely, and support each other in achieving common objectives. Mutual respect ensures that every team member's contributions are valued, fostering a positive and productive atmosphere.

Example:

> At a MacTech Incubator tech startup in Brooklyn, *Jerry Lewis* is part of a cross functional team developing a new mobile app to help college students track their co-curricular involvement. The team includes *Eli Nickel* , the lead engineer; *Nina Dryden*, the UX designer; *Jordan Carlson*, the project manager; and *Maya Thompson*, the marketing strategist.
>
> Each member brings a unique skill set to the table. Eli depends on Nina to deliver intuitive

design mockups that align with the app's functionality. Nina, in turn, relies on Jordan to keep timelines realistic and ensure that feedback loops are built into the process. Maya needs everyone's input to craft messaging that accurately reflects the app's capabilities.

Jerry, a junior developer, is still learning the ropes. She sometimes hesitates to ask questions or clarify expectations, assuming others will fill in the gaps. This leads to a delay in integrating a key feature because she misunderstood the design specs.

During a team retrospective, Jordan gently points out that trust and communication are essential for active collaboration and fostering shared understanding. Jerry realizes that trusting her teammates also means being transparent and proactive in her own role.

In high functioning teams like Jerry's, trust isn't passive, it's built through clear communication, mutual respect, and accountability. When young professionals embrace this mindset early, productivity rises and innovation thrives.

2. Clear Communication

Communication is the engine that drives teamwork. Without effective dialogue, misunderstandings arise, projects suffer, and relationships strain. Teams must establish open channels of communication, actively listen, and provide constructive feedback.

Example:

> At MacTech University, the *RamConnect Marketing Team*, led by *Sandy Bottoms*, with *Don Rickles* handling design, *Aisha Patel* writing content, and *Rachel Kim* overseeing strategy, prepares to launch a fall campaign aimed at increasing alumni engagement through mentoring.
>
> The campaign involves multiple departments:
> - Don needs clear branding guidelines to ensure visual consistency.
> - Aisha must align her messaging with the strategic goals Rachel has outlined.
> - Rachel is responsible for keeping senior leadership updated on progress and ensuring the campaign reflects broader university priorities.
>
> Midway through the project, a miscommunication occurs. Don receives outdated branding assets because Sandy didn't confirm the latest version with the communications office. Meanwhile, Aisha drafts copy that does not reflect the campaign's new focus on career development, as she did not receive a strategy update Rachel shared with leadership.
>
> As a result, the team misses a key internal deadline, delaying the campaign launch and requiring last minute revisions. During a debrief, Rachel emphasizes the importance of

proactive, transparent communication across roles not just within the marketing team, but with external collaborators as well.

In collaborative environments like MacTech's, effective communication between departments is essential. When team members like Sandy, Don, Aisha, and Rachel stay aligned, they not only meet deadlines, they deliver campaigns that reflect the university's mission and resonate with their audience.

3. Shared Goals and Accountability

Teams succeed when all members understand the mission, share common goals, and take ownership of their responsibilities. When individuals feel accountable for their work, productivity increases, and the team thrives.

Example:

> At *MacTech University General Hospital*, a surgical team prepares for a complex cardiac procedure. The team includes *Dr. Lena Morales*, the lead surgeon; *Nipsey Russell, M.D.*, the anesthesiologist; *Katie Cline*, the scrub nurse; and *Dean Martin*, a surgical resident assisting with the operation.
>
> Each member plays a critical role. Dr. Morales relies on Dr. Russell to monitor the patient's vitals and manage anesthesia levels with precision. Donna ensures that all instruments are sterilized and handed off efficiently, while Dean

assists with suturing and keeps track of procedural steps.

Before the surgery begins, the team conducts a "timeout" to confirm the patient's identity, procedure details, and any known risks. Throughout the operation, communication is constant, brief, clear, and purposeful. When Dean hesitates during a step, Dr. Morales calmly guides him, reinforcing the importance of staying focused and encourages Dean to ask for help when he's unsure.

After the successful procedure, the team debriefs. Dr. Morales emphasizes that trust and accountability are non-negotiable in the OR. Every action, from anesthesia to instrument handling, directly impacts patient safety.

By establishing trust, communication, and shared accountability, teams create a strong foundation for success in any workplace.

Managing Different Work Styles and Personalities
A diverse workforce brings together individuals with unique backgrounds, skills, and personalities. While diversity enhances creativity, it also presents challenges in managing different work styles. Understanding how to navigate these differences is essential for a harmonious and productive team.

1. Recognizing Different Work Styles

People approach work in various ways, and teams often include:

➡ Detail-Oriented Thinkers – Prefer structure, data, and precision

➡ Big Picture Innovators - Focus on vision, creativity, and long-term goals.

➡ Process Oriented Planners - Excel at organizing and streamlining workflows.

➡ Spontaneous Problem Solvers - Thrive in fast-paced, flexible environments.

Example:

> At *MacTech University's Office of Communications*, the *Visual Identity Team* is tasked with creating promotional materials for the upcoming "RamConnect Mentorship Week." The team includes *Mona Oswald*, a detail oriented designer known for her pixel perfect layouts, and *Spencer Henry*, a creative lead who thrives on bold concepts and big picture storytelling.
>
> As they begin working on the campaign, Mona focuses on alignment, spacing, and brand consistency, while Spencer pushes for vibrant visuals and unconventional layouts to grab attention. Initially, their approaches seem at odds, Mona worries Spencer's designs stray from MacTech's branding guidelines, while

Spencer feels Mona's edits are too rigid and limit creativity.

During a collaborative review session, their supervisor, *Mary Shelley*, encourages them to recognize each other's strengths. Mona begins to appreciate how Spencer's vision elevates the campaign's emotional impact, while Spencer sees how Mona's precision ensures the final product feels polished and professional.

Together, they refine the materials balancing creativity with consistency and produce a campaign that earns praise from both university leadership and student audiences.

In teams like MacTech's Visual Identity Team, recognizing and valuing different working styles, like Mona's attention to detail and Spencer's creative flair, leads to stronger, more refined outcomes. For young professionals, learning to collaborate across styles is key to producing work that's both innovative and effective.

2. Adapting to Different Personalities

Every workplace consists of different personalities. Some employees are outspoken, while others prefer quiet reflection. Some thrive in collaboration, while others prefer independent work. Managing these differences requires awareness and flexibility.

Example:

> At *MacTech University's Enrollment Marketing Office*, the *Outreach Strategy Team* is preparing for a new campaign to attract prospective students from underrepresented regions.
>
> The team includes *Gary Leonard*, an extroverted outreach coordinator who thrives in high energy environments and excels at building relationships during school visits and virtual info sessions. His teammate, *Mark Cliff*, is a thoughtful and introverted data analyst who prefers working behind the scenes, analyzing enrollment trends and identifying target demographics.
>
> At first, their working styles seem mismatched. Gary moves quickly and improvises, while Mark prefers structure and data backed decisions. But over time, they learn to appreciate each other's strengths. Gary uses Mark's insights to tailor his presentations to specific audiences, while Mark gains a better understanding of how his data is applied in real world interactions.
>
> Their supervisor, *Macy Brooks*, encourages this collaboration by assigning them joint projects that require both outreach and analysis. As a result, the team launches a highly targeted campaign that boosts engagement in key regions by 25%.

By embracing diverse work styles and personalities, teams can maximize productivity and prevent workplace friction.

Tips for Handling Conflicts in Group Settings
No workplace is free of conflict. Disagreements are inevitable, but when managed effectively, they can lead to stronger relationships, improved solutions, and a healthier team environment.

1. Address Conflicts Early

The longer a workplace conflict lingers, the worse it becomes. A proactive approach prevents misunderstandings from escalating into serious issues.

Example:

> At MacTech University's Office of Alumni Relations, *Dwayne Johnson* and *Ken Remsen* are collaborating on a new initiative to boost alumni participation in RamConnect's mentoring program. Dwayne, who favors a high energy, event driven approach, wants to organize a series of in person networking nights. Ken, on the other hand, believes a digital campaign with targeted messaging would be more scalable and cost effective.
>
> As their disagreement grows, both begin working in silos, avoiding direct confrontation. Progress stalls, and their supervisor, *Millie Choi*, notices the tension. She calls a meeting to facilitate a conversation between them.

During the meeting, Millie encourages each to share their reasoning. Dwayne advocates for the power of face to face connection, while Ken presents data showing higher engagement rates from past digital outreach. With Millie's guidance, they find common ground: a hybrid campaign that includes both in person events and a digital follow up strategy.

In teams like MacTech's, early and open communication, especially when disagreements arise, is essential. By discussing their viewpoints and listening to each other, Dwayne and Ken not only resolve their conflict but create a stronger, more inclusive campaign. For young professionals, learning to navigate differences is key to long term success.

2. Maintain Professionalism and Respect

During conflicts, professionalism is key. Employees must remain calm, respectful, and solution focused, rather than letting emotions dictate responses.

Example:

At MacTech University's Office of Alumni Relations, *Alice Han* presents a new slide deck for an upcoming donor engagement event. After the meeting, her colleague *Kevin Delasia* approaches her and says, "I think the presentation missed the mark in terms of storytelling; it felt a bit flat."

Alice feels a bit defensive at first, having spent hours refining the visuals and messaging. But instead of reacting emotionally, she takes a breath and responds constructively:

"Thanks for the feedback, Kevin. Can you clarify which areas you think need improvement? I'd love to make it stronger."

Kevin points out that the donor stories could be more emotionally compelling and suggests adding quotes and photos to personalize the impact. Alice takes the advice, revises the deck, and the final version receives enthusiastic approval from leadership.

In professional settings like MacTech's, responding to criticism with curiosity rather than defensiveness, like Alice did, can turn feedback into an opportunity for growth. Asking for clarification helps shift the conversation from personal critique to collaborative improvement.

3. Focus on Solutions, Not Blame

Effective conflict resolution is about moving forward, not assigning blame. Teams should identify the root cause, propose solutions, and ensure all voices are heard.

Example:

At MacTech University's Office of Student Engagement, *Richard Richardson* and *Carol*

Ann Swift are assigned to co-lead the planning of a large-scale student alumni networking event. As the project progresses, tension builds between them. Both assume the other is responsible for coordinating with the catering vendor, and neither follows up.

When the oversight is discovered during a team check-in, frustration surfaces. Instead of blaming each other, their supervisor, *Patti Cakes*, encourages them to step back and clarify their roles.

Richard and Carol Ann sit down to map out responsibilities. Richard agrees to handle all vendor communications moving forward, while Carol Ann takes the lead on event logistics and volunteer coordination. They also decide to hold brief weekly check-ins to ensure alignment and avoid future confusion.

In collaborative environments like MacTech's, disagreements over task delegation like the one between Richard and Carol Ann can be resolved through open dialogue, role clarification, and proactive planning. For young professionals, learning to address issues early and constructively is key to building trust and delivering successful outcomes.

If two employees argue over task delegation, rather than blaming each other, they could:

1. Clarify roles and responsibilities.
2. Agree on a workflow that benefits both parties.

3. Establish future communication strategies to prevent similar conflicts.

When teams approach conflict with professionalism and open dialogue, they can strengthen relationships rather than damage them.

Final Flex
Teamwork is an essential pillar of workplace success. Strong teams communicate effectively, adapt to diverse personalities, and handle conflicts proactively, leading to higher productivity, stronger relationships, and better decision making. By fostering trust, shared goals, and open communication, employees build collaborative environments that drive innovation and success.

Understanding teamwork isn't just about working together—it's about working smarter, embracing differences, and turning challenges into opportunities. With the right approach, teams can thrive, support one another, and achieve remarkable results in any industry.

Chapter 6: Critical Thinking: The Art of Problem-Solving

Critical thinking is a cornerstone of professional success. This chapter provides a comprehensive guide to mastering analytical reasoning, data interpretation, and systematic problem solving. Here, we will learn how to challenge assumptions, evaluate risks, and make informed decisions that balance short term needs with long term goals. Through practical examples and best practices, the chapter demonstrates how these skills apply across industries, from marketing campaigns to hospital operations, and how they enhance collaboration and innovation. It also explores the evolving role of AI as a tool for research and analysis, stressing the importance of combining machine efficiency with human insight. Concluding with the **SOLVE** Method and interactive exercises, this chapter equips professionals with actionable strategies to think critically, solve complex problems, and thrive in high pressure environments.

In today's fast paced, competitive job market, employers value critical thinking skills.
They look for employees who can solve problems logically and efficiently, adapt to changing circumstances, contribute innovative ideas, and evaluate risks carefully to drive company success. Critical thinking is a skill that sets leaders apart from the rest.

How to Develop Strong Critical Thinking Skills
1. Question Assumptions and Think Critically

Strong critical thinkers don't accept information at face value; they challenge assumptions, ask questions, and seek deeper understanding. Instead of simply following processes, they evaluate whether the methods used are the most effective.

Example:

> At MacTech University's Office of Marketing and Communications, *Bill Frickus*, a marketing analyst, reviews the performance of a recent digital campaign promoting RamConnect's alumni mentoring features. The initial report shows high engagement. Click-through rates are up, and social media shares have doubled compared to the previous campaign.
>
> While the team celebrates the results, Bill takes a more analytical approach. Instead of accepting the numbers at face value, he asks deeper questions:
>
> "Was the spike in engagement driven by ad placement, timing, or the specific audience we targeted? Did one platform outperform the others?"
>
> Bill dives into the data and discovers that a LinkedIn post featuring a testimonial from a recent graduate had significantly higher engagement than other content. He also notices that the campaign performed best among alumni

who graduated within the last five years, suggesting that timing and audience segmentation played a major role.

He shares these insights with the team, helping them refine future campaigns to focus on testimonial driven content and targeted outreach to younger alumni.

In roles like Bill Frickus', curiosity and critical thinking are essential. A marketing analyst reviewing a campaign's success shouldn't just accept reports showing high engagement; they should investigate what specific factors contributed to that success. Was it the ad placement, target audience, or timing? By questioning what drives success, analysts can help their teams make smarter, data informed decisions that lead to even better results.

2. Strengthen Data Interpretation Skills

In many industries, data driven decision making is crucial. Employees must learn how to collect, analyze, and interpret data effectively to support their conclusions.

Example:

At MacTech University General Hospital, *Sherman Fromage*, a financial analyst in the Finance and Budgeting Office, is tasked with evaluating the hospital's quarterly earnings report. The initial figures show a 12% increase in revenue compared to the previous quarter, and several departments are optimistic about the results.

Rather than simply reporting the growth, Sherman digs deeper. He compares the current quarter's performance with historical trends and notices that while revenue is up, operating costs have also risen sharply due to temporary staffing and equipment rentals. He also analyzes external factors, such as a regional uptick in flu cases, that contributed to a surge in patient visits, temporarily boosting revenue.

Sherman presents his findings to leadership, highlighting that while the numbers look positive, the growth may not be sustainable without addressing cost efficiency. He recommends investing in permanent staff and renegotiating vendor contracts to reduce overhead in future quarters.

In roles like Sherman Fromage's, true financial insight comes from looking beyond surface level metrics. By analyzing trends, external influences, and operational costs, financial analysts can provide actionable recommendations that support long term stability and strategic planning.

Best Practices:
- Use data visualization tools to recognize patterns.

- Compare multiple perspectives before making a conclusion.
- Read industry reports to identify emerging trends.

3. Strengthen Logical and Systematic Thinking

Critical thinkers approach problems logically, breaking them down into steps rather than rushing to solutions.

Example:

> At *MacTech University General Hospital*, the internal scheduling system crashes unexpectedly during peak hours, disrupting appointment bookings and staff coordination. *George Burns*, the hospital's senior IT technician, is called in to resolve the issue.

> Rather than immediately restarting the servers, a quick fix that might mask the underlying problem, George takes a systematic approach. He begins by reviewing system logs and error reports, tracing the issue to a recent software update that conflicted with legacy scheduling protocols.

> George runs diagnostic tests, isolates the faulty module, and works with the vendor to patch the software. He also implements a rollback plan and schedules a controlled re-deployment after hours to avoid further disruption. Finally, he documents the incident and updates the hospital's IT protocols to prevent similar crashes in the future.

In high-stakes environments like MacTech University General Hospital, IT technicians like George Burns play a critical role in maintaining operational stability. By relying on logic, evidence, and methodical troubleshooting, not quick fixes, they ensure long term reliability and safeguard essential systems.

By developing analytical questioning, data interpretation, and logical problem solving skills, employees improve efficiency and decision making, making them valuable assets to employers.

Problem-Solving Techniques for Workplace Challenges
Every workplace presents obstacles, from technical difficulties to interpersonal conflicts. Employers need professionals who can approach problems methodically, propose innovative solutions, and execute them effectively. Strong problem solving skills boost productivity and minimize disruptions in the workplace.

1. Identifying the Root Cause of Problems

Many employees rush to fix symptoms of a problem rather than addressing its root cause. That's like a doctor prescribing aspirin to a patient that has a headache without determining the cause. The best problem solvers take the time to investigate the underlying issue before recommending solutions.

Example:

> At *MacTech University General Hospital*, the *Patient Services Team* notices a sudden drop in customer satisfaction ratings on post visit surveys. *Carol Ann Swift*, the Director of Patient Experience, brings the issue to *Richard Richardson*, a problem solving customer service manager known for his analytical approach.
>
> Rather than assuming the drop is due to random fluctuations or isolated complaints, Richard begins a thorough investigation. He reviews recent feedback surveys and notices a recurring theme: long wait times for billing inquiries. He then pulls response time data from the hospital's call center system and finds that average wait times have increased by 40% over the past month.
>
> Digging deeper, Richard examines employee training materials and discovers that several new hires were onboarded without completing the full customer service protocol. He immediately works with *Sherman Fromage*, a financial analyst, to adjust staffing schedules and with *George Burns*, the IT technician, to optimize the call routing system.
>
> Richard also collaborates with Carol Ann to revise the training program and implement a feedback loop for continuous improvement. Within a few weeks, satisfaction scores begin to recover.

In environments like MacTech University General Hospital, professionals like Richard demonstrate that solving service issues requires more than assumptions; it demands a systematic review of data, processes, and people. By identifying root causes and acting on evidence, teams can restore trust and improve the customer experience.

If a company's customer service ratings suddenly drop, rather than assuming it's a random issue, a problem solver would analyze feedback surveys, review response times, and examine employee training materials to pinpoint exactly where improvements are needed.

2. Brainstorming and Creative Problem Solving

Not all solutions come from established formulas. Sometimes, out of the box thinking leads to the best outcomes. Creativity in problem solving helps generate fresh ideas and alternatives.

Example:

At MacTech University General Hospital, *Gary Leonard*, the logistics manager, begins receiving complaints from several departments about delayed deliveries of critical medical supplies. Nurses in the ER report running low on gloves and IV kits, and the surgical team notes that equipment is arriving late, jeopardizing prep times.

Rather than assuming the delays are random or blaming the vendor outright, Gary takes a proactive approach. He reviews delivery logs and notices a pattern: shipments from one distribution center are consistently late. He then examines the hospital's tracking system and realizes it lacks real-time visibility, making it hard to anticipate delays or reroute orders.

Gary organizes a brainstorming session with *George Burns* from IT and *Millie Choi* from procurement. Together, they explore new distribution methods, including partnering with a regional supplier for high-priority items. George recommends investing in a logistics platform that offers real time tracking and automated alerts, while Millie begins renegotiating vendor contracts to include performance benchmarks.

Within a month, delivery times improve, and supply shortages decrease significantly.

In roles like Gary Leonard's, solving logistical challenges requires more than quick fixes—it demands data analysis, cross-functional collaboration, and strategic investment. By identifying root causes and implementing targeted solutions, Gary ensures the hospital's supply chain supports patient care without disruption.

A logistics manager struggling with slow deliveries might brainstorm new distribution methods, invest in technology that streamlines tracking, or negotiate new vendor contracts to optimize supply chain efficiency.

Best Practices:

- Approach challenges with multiple solutions instead of settling on the first option.
- Consider long term impacts rather than temporary fixes.
- Collaborate with colleagues for diverse perspectives.

3. Staying Calm and Strategic Under Pressure

Strong problem solvers don't panic when faced with challenges. They remain calm, organized, and adaptable in high pressure situations.

Example:

> At MacTech University General Hospital's Billing Department, *Erika Ramstein*, a customer service representative, receives a call from *Barb Dwyer*, a longtime patient who is upset about a recent billing error. Barb is frustrated and raises her voice, saying she's been charged twice for the same outpatient procedure and hasn't received a clear explanation.
>
> Instead of reacting emotionally or becoming defensive, Erika listens carefully and lets Barb finish speaking. She calmly responds:
>
> "I understand how frustrating this must be, Ms. Dwyer, and I appreciate you bringing it to our attention. Let me take a closer look at your

account and see what may have caused the duplicate charge."

Erika reviews the billing records, identifies the error, and explains the situation clearly. He assures Barb that the duplicate charge will be reversed and offers to send a confirmation email with the corrected invoice. She also provides a direct contact number in case she has further questions.

Barb, initially angry, ends the call feeling heard and respected.

In high pressure roles like Erika's, professionalism and empathy are key—as is problem solving. By staying calm, listening actively, analyzing root causes, and offering clear solutions, employees can turn difficult interactions into opportunities to strengthen trust and preserve the organization's reputation.

Evaluating Risks and Making Sound Decisions
Every professional, regardless of industry, must evaluate risks and make informed decisions. Employers seek employees who are proactive, strategic, and capable of weighing consequences before taking action. Poor decision making can lead to costly mistakes, while strong risk assessment helps avoid unnecessary setbacks.

1. Assessing Short Term vs. Long Term Risks

Strong decision makers consider both immediate outcomes and long term effects before making choices.

Example:

> At MacTech University General Hospital, the Operations Strategy Team debates investing in a new inventory management system to streamline the tracking of medical supplies. *Patti Cakes*, the Director of Operations, is enthusiastic about the long-term benefits, while *Vincent Pots*, the Finance Manager, is concerned about the upfront costs.
>
> The proposed system would require a significant investment:
>
> - Short term costs include purchasing the software, upgrading hardware, and training staff across multiple departments.
> - Long term benefits could include reduced waste, faster restocking, improved patient care, fewer delays, and higher staff satisfaction.
>
> To make an informed decision, *Sherman Fromage*, a financial analyst, conducts a cost-benefit analysis comparing current inefficiencies with projected savings over the next five years. Meanwhile, *George Burns*, the hospital's IT technician, evaluates the system's compatibility

with existing infrastructure and estimates the implementation timeline.

After reviewing the data, the team agrees to pilot the system in one department before scaling hospital-wide. The decision balances financial caution with strategic innovation.

In organizations like MacTech University General Hospital, decisions about technology investments require collaboration across roles. By weighing short term costs against long term gains and involving experts like Vincent, Patti, Sherman, and George, the team ensures their choices are both fiscally responsible and forward thinking.

A company debating whether to invest in new technology must weigh short term costs and long term benefits. By analyzing both short and long term impacts, decision makers ensure they invest wisely instead of rushing into risky spending.

2. Gathering Information Before Making Decisions

The best professionals don't guess. They research thoroughly, consult experts, and assess multiple options before finalizing a decision.

Example:

At MacTech University General Hospital, *Mary Shelley*, the hiring manager for the Patient Services Department, is tasked with selecting a new coordinator to oversee front desk operations and patient intake.

After interviewing several candidates, Mary identifies one standout applicant, *Katie Cline*, who displays confident communication and polished presentation skills. However, Mary knows that interviews alone don't tell the full story.

She reviews Katie's past work experience and notices strong performance in similar roles at two regional clinics. Mary then contacts Katie's references, including *Richard Richardson*, a former supervisor, who praises Katie's reliability but notes she struggled with adapting to new software systems. To dig deeper, Mary asks Katie to complete a short job assessment focused on scheduling and data entry accuracy.

The results show Katie has improved her technical skills significantly, and her attention to detail is well above average. With a comprehensive understanding of Katie's abilities, including interview performance, experience, reference feedback, and assessment results, Mary confidently moves forward with the hire.

In roles like Mary's, making a smart hiring decision means going beyond first impressions. Hiring managers ensure they select candidates who are both personable and capable by combining interviews with data backed evaluations, reviewing past experiences, references, and job assessments.

Best Practices:
- Gather data from reliable sources before committing to decisions.
- Evaluate potential risks logically instead of emotionally.
- Seek advice from trusted mentors or leaders.

3. Understanding When to Take Calculated Risks

Risk is a natural part of business, but smart professionals take calculated risks rather than impulsive ones.

Example:

> At *RamReach*, a MacTech University affiliated startup focused on alumni engagement technology, founder *Ken Remsen* considers expanding the company's services to include a mobile app for student mentorship tracking.
>
> Before moving forward, Ken gathers his leadership team, *Spencer Henry* from finance, *Alice Han* from operations, and *Maya Thompson* from marketing, to evaluate the risks and opportunities.
>
> - Financial risks: Spencer points out that developing the app would require a six figure investment, including hiring a mobile development team and onboarding new support staff. He asks,

"Can we afford this without compromising our current operations?"
- Market risks: Maya conducts a competitive analysis and surveys current users. While there's interest in mobile access, she notes that several competitors already offer similar features. "Is there enough demand for *our* version to stand out?" she asks.
- Operational risks: Alice raises concerns about internal capacity. "Do we have the infrastructure and team bandwidth to support a new product line while maintaining our current platform?"

Ken listens carefully and proposes a phased approach: launching a pilot version of the app with a select group of MacTech students and alumni. This allows the team to test demand, gather feedback, and manage costs before committing to a full-scale rollout.

For startup founders like Ken Remsen, expansion isn't just about ambition, it's about strategic planning. By weighing financial, market, and operational risks with input from trusted team members, leaders can make informed decisions that support sustainable growth.

A startup founder expanding their business must consider:

- Financial risks - Can the company afford growth?
- Market risks - Is there enough demand?
- Operational risks - Do employees have the resources to succeed?

By carefully weighing risks, professionals maximize opportunities while minimizing potential failures.

AI and Critical Thinking: Working Smarter with Technology

Artificial Intelligence is transforming how we work, learn, and solve problems. But AI is not a replacement for human thinking, it's an enhancement tool. The most successful professionals will be those who know how to combine machine efficiency with human insight.

Using AI Tools for Research and Analysis

AI can help professionals gather data, summarize reports, and identify patterns faster than ever. Tools like ChatGPT, Google Bard, and AI powered dashboards can assist with:

- Market research
- Drafting reports
- Analyzing customer feedback
- Generating ideas for campaigns or presentations

Example:

> At MacTech University's Career Services Office, *Hollie Schitt* uses an AI writing assistant to draft a student guide on internship

preparation. She then edits the content, considering the university's tone, and adds real student testimonials. The AI helped her save time, but her human judgment made the final product authentic and relevant.

When to Trust AI vs. Human Judgment
AI is powerful, but it's not perfect. It can make mistakes, reflect biases, or miss context. Professionals must know when to rely on AI and when to step in with human reasoning.

Example:

> *Sherman Fromage*, a financial analyst, uses an AI tool to forecast budget trends. The tool suggests cutting staff to reduce costs. Sherman knows this would hurt patient care, so he adjusts the model to prioritize efficiency without sacrificing service. His human insight ensures the decision aligns with values and goals.

Best Practices:
- Use AI for speed and structure, not final decisions
- Always fact check AI generated content
- Apply ethical judgment when interpreting data
- Ask: *Does this make sense in the real world?*

Critical Evaluation of AI Generated Content
Don't accept AI output at face value. Ask:

- What sources did this come from?
- Is the tone appropriate for my audience?
- Are there gaps or assumptions I need to address?

Example:

> *Bill Frickus* receives an AI-generated summary of alumni engagement data. It looks promising, but he notices the report overlooks key metrics like retention and repeat participation. He adds those manually and presents a more complete picture to leadership.

Combining Human Insight with Machine Processing
The future of work is human + machine, not human vs. machine. Professionals who can interpret AI results, ask better questions, and apply emotional intelligence will lead the way.

The SOLVE Method: A Framework for Smart Problem Solving

Introducing a practical, step by step approach to critical thinking and decision making:

S - Scrutinize the Problem

Don't jump to conclusions. Ask: What's really going on here? What are the symptoms vs. the root causes?

O - Organize Information

Gather relevant data, feedback, and context. Use charts, timelines, or summaries to make sense of it.

L - List Possible Solutions

Brainstorm multiple options. Think creatively and include both conventional and out of the box ideas.

V - Vet Each Option

Evaluate pros and cons. Consider risks, resources, and long term impact. Consult others if needed.

E - Execute and Evaluate

Choose the best path, take action, and monitor results. Be ready to pivot if needed.

Example:

> At *RamReach*, a student engagement startup, the team faces declining app usage. Using the SOLVE Method:
>
> - **S**crutinize the Problem - They identify the root issue: students find the interface confusing.
> - **O**rganize Information - They gather feedback from users and review analytics.
> - **L**ist possible solutions - They brainstorm redesigns, tutorials, and gamification features.
> - **V**et Each Option - They test each idea with a pilot group.
> - **E**xecute and Evaluate - They launch the new version and track engagement weekly.

The result? A 60% increase in active users within two months.

Critical Thinking Exercises
- Reverse Brainstorming: Instead of asking "How do we solve this?" ask "How could we make this worse?" Then reverse those ideas.
- Devil's Advocate: Challenge your own assumptions. What if the opposite were true?
- Scenario Mapping: Imagine best-case, worst-case, and most likely outcomes. Plan for each.

Final Flex
Critical thinking is one of the most valuable skills employers seek in new employees. Strong analytical thinkers can break down problems, evaluate data, and make sound decisions that enhance productivity. By mastering problem solving techniques, risk evaluation, and effective decision making, early career professionals increase their career success while driving workplace efficiency and innovation.

Employers don't just want employees who follow instructions. They want critical thinkers who add value, adapt to challenges, and contribute innovative solutions. Developing these skills sets professionals apart, making them indispensable in any industry.

Chapter 7: Professionalism: Building a Strong Reputation

This chapter explores the concept of professionalism as a critical factor in career success. It emphasizes that professionalism extends beyond appearance to include demeanor, work ethic, integrity, and accountability. Key topics include workplace etiquette, effective communication, appropriate dress codes, and digital professionalism. The chapter also addresses managing workplace relationships, resolving conflicts, and maintaining ethical behavior. Practical examples and best practices illustrate how professionals can build trust, credibility, and a strong reputation in both physical and virtual environments. Ultimately, professionalism is portrayed as a blend of character, competence, and consistency that drives long term success.

Professionalism is more than dressing appropriately. It's about demeanor, work ethic, and integrity.

Why Employers Prioritize Professionalism in Candidates
Professionalism is a cornerstone of career success, influencing how employees are perceived, how effectively they contribute to their organizations, and how well they build relationships in the workplace. Employers value candidates who take their careers seriously, demonstrating a strong work ethic, respect, and accountability. Beyond technical skills, hiring

managers seek individuals who can navigate workplace dynamics with integrity, etiquette, grace, and professionalism.

The Fundamentals of Workplace Etiquette

Workplace etiquette refers to the behaviors and practices that foster respectful, efficient, and productive professional environments. Individuals who exhibit proper etiquette help maintain harmony, reduce conflicts, and create positive impressions on colleagues, clients, and leadership.

1. Respecting Colleagues and Office Norms

Respect is the foundation of workplace etiquette. Employees must honor colleagues' time, space, and opinions, ensuring collaborative and effective interactions.

Example:

> At MacTech University's Office of Alumni Relations, *Norman Scott* , a newly hired program assistant, attends his first weekly team meeting. The group, led by *Raych Nair*, with team members *Sandy Bottoms*, *Ken Remsen*, and *Don Rickles*, is discussing plans for the upcoming RamConnect Mentorship Week.

> As ideas begin to flow, Norman listens attentively, jotting down notes and observing how each team member contributes. When he suggests measures to improving the event's

registration process, he waits until the current speaker finishes before raising his hand and sharing his thoughts.

Raych notices his respectful approach, and later commends Norman for his professionalism and thoughtful input. Norman's behavior helps foster a collaborative atmosphere, encouraging open dialogue and mutual respect among the team.

Instead of interrupting while others speak, team members actively listen, take notes, and wait for their turn to contribute. This behavior fosters a respectful dialogue, encouraging open discussions and mutual consideration.

2. Professional Communication

Effective workplace communication balances clarity, politeness, and appropriateness across different formats whether verbal, written, or nonverbal.

Example:

At MacTech University's Office of Alumni Relations, *Richard Richardson*, a summer intern, is tasked with drafting a follow-up email to his supervisor, *Raych Nair*, regarding logistics for an upcoming RamConnect event.

Eager to show initiative, Richard quickly writes the email but pauses before hitting send. Instead of rushing, he reviews the message carefully. He begins with a professional greeting:

Subject: Follow Up on RamConnect Event Logistics

Dear Ms. Nair,

I hope you're having a great start to the week. I wanted to follow up on the venue confirmation for the RamConnect Mentorship Mixer. I've reached out to the facilities team and am awaiting their response. I'll keep you updated as soon as I hear back.

Please let me know if there's anything else I should prioritize this week.

Best regards,
Richard

An intern drafting an email to their supervisor should use a professional greeting, maintain a clear and respectful tone, and proofread before sending rather than rushing to submit a poorly structured message. Thoughtful communication shows professionalism and attention to detail.

Best Practices:

- Use courteous language in workplace conversations.
- Avoid overly casual or unprofessional emails when speaking to management.
- Adapt communication style to formal or informal settings appropriately.

3. Dress Code and Personal Presentation

Workplace attire contributes to professionalism. Dressing appropriately for the work environment, whether corporate formal or business casual, reflects respect for company culture and expectations. You can never be dressed too well!

Example:

> At MacTech University's Office of Strategic Partnerships, *Jordan Carlson*, a newly hired outreach coordinator, is scheduled to attend a client presentation with *Carol Ann Swift*, the department's associate director. The meeting is with representatives from a major donor foundation considering a multi-year gift to support RamConnect's expansion.
>
> Knowing the importance of first impressions, Jordan chooses a tailored blazer, dress slacks, and polished shoes; attire that aligns with the university's business standards. Carol Ann notices his effort and appreciates that he's taken the occasion seriously.
>
> During the presentation, Jordan's professional appearance complements his confident demeanor and thoughtful contributions. The foundation representatives comment on the team's preparedness and professionalism, reinforcing MacTech's credibility.
>
> For employees like Jordan, dressing appropriately for client-facing events isn't just

about style, it's about signaling respect, competence, and readiness. Professional attire helps reinforce trust and ensures individuals are perceived as serious and capable in their roles.

When an employee attending a client presentation chooses professional attire that aligns with business standards, they reinforce credibility and confidence. Dressing appropriately ensures employees are perceived as capable and serious about their roles.

The Evolution of Casual Friday
Casual Friday used to mean jeans and sneakers. Today, workplace dress codes are more flexible but that doesn't mean anything goes. The key is to be relaxed, not sloppy.

Modern Guidelines:

- Smart casual wins - Think clean jeans, polos, sweaters, or casual dresses.
- Know your audience - If you're meeting with clients or leadership, elevate your look.
- Avoid extremes - Ripped clothing, graphic tees, or overly trendy outfits can send the wrong message.
- Ask when unsure - If you're new to a company, observe what others wear or ask HR for guidance.

Example:

> At MacTech's Innovation Lab, Fridays are casual but when *Jalen Smith* has a surprise

meeting with a donor, he swaps his hoodie for a
button down and blazer. He's still comfortable,
but he's also prepared.

Industry Specific Style Guides
Not all industries dress the same. What's appropriate in
finance may feel out of place in tech or the arts.
Understanding your field's norms shows cultural
awareness and professionalism.

General Style Cues:

- Finance, Law, Consulting - Conservative,
  tailored, and polished.
- Tech, Startups, Creative Fields - Smart casual,
  expressive but clean.
- Healthcare, Education, Nonprofits - Practical,
  approachable, and neat.
- Media, Fashion, Design - Trend forward, brand
  conscious, and intentional.

Tip: When in doubt, dress one level up from what you
expect others to wear, especially for interviews or first
impressions. You can always tell interviewers you are
heading somewhere better after your meeting
concludes!

Cost-Effective Professional Wardrobe Building
Looking professional doesn't have to break the bank.
With a few smart choices, you can build a wardrobe
that's versatile, affordable, and aligned with your goals.

Strategies:

- Start with basics - A blazer, neutral slacks, a white button down, and clean shoes go a long way.
- Mix and match - Choose pieces that can be worn in multiple combinations.
- Shop smart - Thrift stores, outlet malls, and online sales offer great deals.
- Invest in fit - Tailoring inexpensive clothes can make them look high end.
- Borrow or swap - Consider clothing swaps with friends or borrowing for special events.

Example:

> *Charles Wilson*, a first gen college student, builds his wardrobe with three core outfits from a local thrift store. He mixes in a few new pieces from online sales and tailors a blazer for $20. He's confident, polished, and interview ready, without overspending.

Video Call Appearance Standards
In hybrid and remote work environments, your video call presence is part of your professional brand. Just because you're working from home doesn't mean standards disappear, if anything, they evolve.

Example:

> During a virtual pitch to a potential employer, *Maya Thompson* logs in from her apartment. She's wearing a blazer over a simple top, her

background is tidy, and her lighting is bright and even. Her professional setup helps her stand out and she lands the internship.

Best Practices:

- Dress for the role - Wear attire that matches the meeting's tone. A collared shirt or blouse is often a safe bet, even if you're not in a full suit.
- Check your background - A clean, neutral space or virtual background keeps the focus on you.
- Mind the lighting - Natural light or a ring light can make a big difference. Avoid sitting with your back to a window.
- Frame yourself well - Position your camera at eye level and center yourself in the frame.
- Minimize distractions - Silence notifications, close unnecessary tabs, and let others in your space know you're on a call.

Digital Professionalism: Building Your Online Reputation with Purpose

In today's connected world, your digital presence is often your first impression. Before an interview, a networking call, or even a coffee chat, someone may Google your name, scroll through your LinkedIn, or glance at your Instagram. What they find matters.

Digital professionalism is about showing up online with intention, consistency, and credibility. It's not about being perfect, it's about being authentic, respectful, and aligned with your career goals.

Social Media Audit Checklist
Before you build your brand, you need to know what's already out there. A social media audit helps you take control of your digital footprint.

Checklist:

- Google your name. What comes up? Is it accurate and professional?
- Review your public profiles (LinkedIn, Instagram, TikTok, Twitter/X).
- Remove or archive posts that don't reflect your values or goals.
- Update bios and profile pictures to reflect your current identity.
- Check privacy settings, know what's public and what's private.
- Search old usernames or tagged photos. Clean up where needed.

Tip: You don't need to delete your personality, just make sure your public facing content supports your professional story.

Online Reputation Management
Your reputation isn't just what you say, it's what others see, share, and remember. Managing it means being proactive, not reactive.

Example:

> *Macy Brooks*, a recent graduate, notices a tagged photo from a college party circulating on social media. She politely asks the friend to

remove the tag and updates her privacy settings. Meanwhile, she posts a LinkedIn article about her internship experience, shifting the narrative to her professional growth.

Best Practices:

- Respond professionally to comments, even when disagreeing.
- Avoid venting about work, school, or colleagues online.
- Share achievements, insights, and helpful resources.
- Engage with others' content thoughtfully, likes, comments, and reposts matter.
- Monitor mentions and tags regularly.

Digital Networking Etiquette

Networking online is powerful but it requires tact. Whether you're messaging someone on LinkedIn or joining a virtual event, your approach matters.

Do:

- Personalize connection requests ("I enjoyed your talk on career pivots, would love to stay in touch.")
- Be respectful of time, keep messages concise and purposeful.
- Follow up with gratitude ("Thanks for the advice, your insights helped me prepare for my interview.")
- Engage with others' posts before asking for favors.

Don't:

- Send generic messages ("Hi, let's connect.")
- Ask for jobs or referrals without building rapport.
- Spam comment sections or group chats.

Example:

> *Hollie Schitt* attends a virtual alumni panel. After the event, she messages one of the speakers:
>
> "Hi Claudia, I really appreciated your advice on navigating early career transitions. I'm exploring roles in UX and would love to connect and learn more about your journey."
>
> Claudia responds and a mentorship begins.

Personal Brand Consistency Across Platforms
Your personal brand is the story you tell across LinkedIn, Instagram, TikTok, your resume, and even your email signature. Consistency builds trust.

Example:

> *Taylor Morgan*, a Gen Z career coach, uses LinkedIn to share job search tips, TikTok to post short videos on resume hacks, and Instagram to highlight student success stories. Her tone is friendly, her visuals are clean, and her message is consistent: she helps young professionals thrive.

Best Practices:

- Use similar profile photos and bios across platforms.
- Highlight the same core values and strengths.
- Share content that reflects your interests and expertise.
- Avoid contradictions, don't say you're passionate about sustainability on LinkedIn and post wasteful behavior on Instagram.

Managing Workplace Relationships with Professionalism

Workplace success is not just about individual accomplishments. It's about how well employees collaborate, resolve conflicts, and maintain positive relationships. Professionalism plays a crucial role in fostering healthy team dynamics, trust, and collaboration.

1. Building Positive and Productive Relationships

Maintaining strong workplace relationships requires effective teamwork, respect for colleagues' perspectives, and open collaboration.

Example:

At MacTech University's Office of Student Success, *Ziggy Cleveland*, a data analyst from Institutional Research, and *Grover Young*, a program coordinator from the Career Center, are assigned to collaborate on a new dashboard for tracking student engagement through RamConnect.

Ziggy approaches the project with a data first mindset, focusing on metrics, backend integration, and predictive modeling. Grover, on the other hand, prioritizes usability and student facing features, wanting the dashboard to be intuitive and visually engaging.

Initially, their approaches seem to clash. Ziggy questions the need for design heavy elements, while Grover worries that the dashboard might be too technical for everyday users. Instead of dismissing each other's perspectives, they schedule a working session to align their goals.

They openly discuss their priorities, compromise on certain features, and agree to build a prototype that balances functionality with accessibility. Throughout the process, they maintain transparent communication, share updates regularly, and consult with stakeholders to ensure the final product meets both technical and user experience standards.

The result is a dashboard that is user-friendly and informative, delivering robust data insights with an intuitive interface. Ziggy and Grover earn praise from their leadership and improve engagement tracking across departments.

When employees like Ziggy and Grover embrace collaboration and respect each other's expertise, they turn potential conflict into innovation. Open dialogue, compromise, and clear communication lead to stronger outcomes and lasting professional relationships.

Best Practices:
- Show appreciation for colleagues' contributions.
- Encourage open dialogue and constructive feedback.
- Foster an environment where differences are valued rather than opposed.

2. Navigating Workplace Conflicts Professionally

Workplace disagreements are inevitable, but handling them professionally prevents unnecessary tension and maintains a positive work culture.

Example:

> During a cross departmental initiative at MacTech University, *Maria Chen*, a Career Center coordinator, and *James Kittlesworth*, a DAUR communications strategist, found themselves at odds over project priorities. Aiming to enhance alumni engagement through RamConnect, Maria wanted to integrate alumni-student mentoring features, while James prioritized launching a marketing campaign.

> Instead of letting the disagreement escalate, they scheduled a one on one meeting to discuss their perspectives. In the conversation, Maria explained how student engagement metrics showed a need for stronger mentoring tools,

while James shared data indicating alumni interest was highest during campaign launches.

By listening to each other's viewpoints, they identified a shared goal: increasing meaningful connections between students and alumni. They agreed to phase the project. First, enhancing mentoring features, then launching the campaign with those improvements as a key selling point.

This approach not only resolved the conflict but strengthened their collaboration. Their ability to engage in professional conflict resolution prevented resentment and fostered a more constructive, team oriented atmosphere.

Best Practices:
- Address conflicts calmly and objectively, avoiding emotional outbursts.
- Focus on solutions, not blame.
- Seek mediation when necessary to ensure fairness.

3. Maintaining Ethical Workplace Behavior

Professional relationships require trust and ethical interactions. Employees must behave with honesty, discretion, and reliability in their interactions.

Example:

While working late in the MacTech University Career Center, *Alicia Rivers*, a student engagement coordinator, overheard a conversation between two senior administrators discussing upcoming changes to staffing and budget allocations, information that hadn't yet been shared publicly.

Recognizing the sensitivity of the topic, Alicia chose not to repeat or speculate about what she heard, even when colleagues casually asked if she knew anything about the rumored changes. Instead, she continued to focus on her work and waited for official communications from leadership.

By respecting workplace confidentiality, Alicia demonstrated a strong sense of ethical responsibility and professionalism. Her discretion helped maintain trust within the organization and ensured that sensitive information was handled appropriately.

Managing workplace relationships professionally strengthens trust, collaboration, and team efficiency, making employees more valuable to their organizations.

Accountability and Integrity in Professional Settings
Employers prioritize accountability and integrity, as they indicate reliability and ethical responsibility. Employees who take ownership of their actions, uphold honesty, and consistently follow ethical standards contribute to a trustworthy and productive workplace.

1. Taking Ownership of Responsibilities

Employees must own their tasks, meet deadlines, and fulfill obligations reliably. Accountability ensures workplace efficiency and reduces disruptions.

Example:

> During the rollout of a new alumni engagement dashboard for RamConnect, *Daniel Rivera*, the project manager from the DAUR tech team, encountered unexpected delays due to a third party API integration issue. The delay meant the dashboard wouldn't be ready in time for a scheduled demonstration to university leadership.
>
> Rather than shifting blame to the vendor or his team, Daniel took full responsibility. He immediately informed stakeholders, including *Lisa Knight*, the Director of Alumni Engagement, and *Alice Han*, the Career Center liaison, explaining the obstacle and the solution strategies.
>
> Daniel proposed a revised timeline, offered to provide a temporary workaround for the demo, and scheduled regular updates to keep everyone informed. His transparency and solution-oriented approach reassured the team and preserved trust, transforming a potential setback into a leadership opportunity for himself, and a collaborative one for his team. Instead of shifting blame, Daniel accepted responsibility, communicated transparently, and offered

solutions to minimize impact, demonstrating exemplary professional accountability.

Best Practices:

- Follow through on commitments without excuses.
- Take initiative in addressing mistakes rather than avoiding responsibility.
- Communicate openly when challenges arise instead of waiting until problems escalate.

2. Demonstrating Integrity and Honesty

Integrity means staying truthful, ethical, and fair in professional dealings, even when faced with challenges.

Example:

> While reviewing quarterly budget reports for the MacTech University Career Center, *Priya Desai*, a recently hired financial analyst, noticed a discrepancy in the allocation totals for a student engagement initiative. The numbers didn't match the approved budget from the previous month.
>
> Although she was new to the team and unsure if it was her place to raise the issue, Priya chose to bring it to the attention of her supervisor, *Mark Cliff*, the Director of Finance. After reviewing the report, Mark confirmed that a formula error had caused the miscalculation, an issue that, concerns if left unaddressed, could have led to overspending and compliance.

Priya then worked with Mark to correct the report and implement a double check process for future submissions. Her honesty and initiative not only prevented potential complications but also earned her the respect of her colleagues.

This example highlights how professional integrity builds trust and credibility. It also reinforces an important message for new employees: you can never be faulted for politely pointing out inaccuracies. Speaking up, especially when done respectfully, shows commitment to the organization's success.

Best Practices:
- Be honest in communication and decision making.
- Uphold ethical standards, even in difficult situations.
- Avoid cutting corners or misrepresenting facts for personal gain.

3. Aligning Actions with Company Values

Professionals must ensure their behavior aligns with workplace values and culture, contributing positively to the organization's reputation.

Example:

At MacTech University's Office of Alumni Relations, *Kevin Delasia*, a program coordinator, was managing inquiries related to a new alumni benefits portal. One afternoon, an alumnus called in frustrated about login issues and missing profile data. The caller was impatient and raised their voice, clearly upset.

Instead of reacting defensively or brushing off the complaint, Kevin remained calm and professional. He listened carefully, acknowledged the frustration, and assured the alumnus that their concerns would be addressed promptly. Kevin then coordinated with the IT team to resolve the issue and followed up personally with the alumnus to confirm everything was working correctly.

Kevin's patience and professionalism not only resolved the issue but also left the alumnus feeling heard and valued. Had Jordan responded negatively or dismissed the concern, it could have damaged the university's reputation and trust with its alumni community.

A company emphasizing customer satisfaction expects employees to address customer concerns with professionalism and patience. This example illustrates how ethical conduct and a commitment to customer satisfaction contribute to long term success. It also serves as a reminder, especially for new employees, that addressing concerns with respect and care strengthens relationships and reflects positively on the organization, while ignoring complaints or reacting negatively harms the company's image.

Accountability and integrity strengthen workplace credibility, helping employees build trust, respect, and long term career success.

Final Flex

Employers prioritize professionalism, accountability, and workplace etiquette—traits that directly impact team efficiency, company reputation, and overall productivity. Candidates who take their careers seriously and demonstrate professionalism become valuable assets to organizations, contributing to a positive work culture, ethical business practices, and long term success.

Mastering workplace etiquette, building professional relationships, and maintaining integrity helps professionals thrive in their roles, creating lasting career opportunities and leadership potential.

Employers don't just hire for skills. They hire for character, professionalism, and the ability to contribute meaningfully to the workplace.

Chapter 8: Equity & Inclusion: Strengthening Workplace Culture

This chapter emphasizes the critical role of Diversity, Equity, and Inclusion (DEI) in shaping modern workplace culture. It explains that DEI is not just a moral imperative but a business necessity that drives innovation, collaboration, and employee engagement. The chapter explores why DEI matters, highlighting its impact on creativity, fairness, and retention, and provides real world examples of inclusive practices in action. It also outlines how employees can advocate for inclusivity through collaboration, supporting Employee Resource Groups (ERGs), and addressing unconscious bias. Finally, it offers strategies for recognizing and reducing bias, ensuring equitable opportunities for all employees, and fostering psychological safety as a foundation for long term success.

Diversity, equity, and inclusion (DEI) initiatives are increasingly shaping workplace culture. Employers expect professionals to embrace inclusivity, understand different perspectives, and contribute to a positive work environment.

The Importance of Diversity, Equity, and Inclusion (DEI) in the Workplace
Diversity, Equity, and Inclusion (DEI) are not just buzzwords. They are essential components of a thriving and competitive organization. Businesses that prioritize inclusion benefit from greater innovation, stronger

collaboration, and enhanced employee engagement, leading to increased productivity and long term success.

Employers seek professionals who actively contribute to inclusive workplace cultures, advocate for fairness, and recognize unconscious biases that may affect decision making. Understanding why DEI matters, how employees can promote inclusivity, and how to address biases helps individuals create healthier, more effective workplaces.

At their core, Diversity, Equity, and Inclusion (DEI) strategies ensure that all individuals are given equal opportunity, regardless of their race, gender, background, ability, or any other aspect of identity. DEI should never be used as a tool to exclude individuals based on a perceived lack of diversity, nor should it serve as a mechanism to reward others solely for their identity.

Instead, DEI should foster environments where everyone is treated with fairness, dignity, and respect. It's about removing barriers, not creating new ones. When implemented ethically and thoughtfully, DEI strengthens organizations by promoting collaboration, innovation, and trust, ensuring that all voices are heard and valued.

Why DEI Matters in the Modern Workforce
Diversity, equity, and inclusion initiatives are crucial for fostering a workplace that values individuals from all backgrounds, identities, and experiences. Organizations that prioritize DEI do more than just

comply with legal requirements. They empower employees and enhance business performance.

1. Inclusion Drives Innovation and Creativity

A diverse workforce brings multiple perspectives and new ways of thinking, encouraging innovation. Employees with varied backgrounds, cultural experiences, and skills contribute unique ideas, allowing companies to solve problems more effectively.

Example:

> At MacTech University, the DAUR marketing team was tasked with promoting a new global alumni networking initiative through RamConnect. The team included *Sofia Torres*, originally from Argentina; *Kenji Watanabe*, who grew up in Japan; and *Amina Adebayo*, a first generation Nigerian American. Each brought unique cultural insights to the table.
>
> As they developed the campaign, their varied perspectives helped shape messaging that resonated across regions. Sofia emphasized the importance of storytelling and emotional connection for Latin American audiences. Kenji suggested a more minimalist and formal tone for East Asian markets, while Amina advocated for vibrant visuals and community driven language that would appeal to African and diaspora communities.
>
> By integrating these diverse viewpoints, the team created a campaign that felt inclusive and

authentic to alumni around the world.
Engagement rates increased significantly, and
feedback from international alumni highlighted
how seen and valued they felt.

This example illustrates how cultural diversity within a team can directly enhance the effectiveness of global outreach. When embraced thoughtfully, it leads to stronger connections, better outcomes, and a more inclusive brand identity.

2. Equity Promotes Fairness and Opportunity

Equity ensures that all employees receive fair treatment, access to opportunities, and the resources needed to succeed. This includes addressing systemic barriers that prevent certain groups from advancing professionally.

Example:

> At MacTech University, the Human Resources team conducted a review of promotion practices across administrative departments. Led by *Robert Locke*, the Director of HR, and *Malik Hawes*, the Diversity and Inclusion Officer, the team discovered a concerning trend: women and employees from underrepresented backgrounds were significantly less likely to hold leadership roles, despite having comparable qualifications and performance evaluations to their peers.
>
> Rather than ignoring the findings, Robert and Malik presented the data to senior leadership and proposed a strategic response. They

launched a university wide mentorship initiative, pairing emerging talent with experienced leaders, and introduced targeted leadership development workshops designed to prepare all employees, regardless of background, for advancement opportunities.

One standout participant, *Jasmine Ortiz*, a program coordinator in the Career Center, credited the mentorship program with helping her build the confidence and skills needed to apply for a managerial role. Within a year, she was promoted to Assistant Director.

This initiative not only improved representation in leadership but also reinforced MacTech's commitment to equity and inclusion. By addressing systemic barriers and creating pathways for growth, the university ensured that career advancement was based on merit and opportunity, not background.

A company reviewing promotion practices discovers that women and minorities are less likely to be in leadership roles, despite having similar qualifications. By implementing mentorship programs and leadership training, they ensure equitable access to career growth opportunities.

3. Inclusion Strengthens Workplace Culture and Employee Retention

Employees who feel valued, respected, and included are more engaged, satisfied, and committed to their organizations. Inclusive workplaces experience higher retention rates, stronger team collaboration, and increased job satisfaction.

Example:

> At MacTech University's Division of Alumni and University Relations (DAUR), the communications team prepared for a major campaign to reintroduce RamConnect to alumni across generations. The team included *Luis Hernandez*, a first generation college graduate; *Mei Ru Liu*, an international staff member from China; and *Tasha Greene*, a long time MacTech alumna and staff member.
>
> During a brainstorming session, Mei hesitated to share her ideas, unsure if her perspective would resonate. Sensing this, Tasha, who was leading the meeting, made a point to invite input from everyone and emphasized that all voices were valued. Luis then shared how his own background shaped his understanding of alumni engagement, which encouraged Mei to speak up about how cultural nuances could influence messaging for international alumni.
>
> The open and respectful environment allowed for a rich exchange of ideas. The final campaign reflected a broader range of experiences and perspectives, resulting in stronger engagement metrics and positive feedback from alumni across regions.

This example shows how an inclusive work culture, where employees feel safe to share their thoughts without fear of exclusion or judgment, leads to better collaboration, innovation, and trust. Psychological safety isn't just a buzzword; it's a foundation for meaningful work and long term success.

DEI is not just a moral imperative. It is a business necessity. Companies that invest in DEI create environments that support employees, boost innovation, and strengthen long term success.

How Employees Can Advocate for Inclusivity
Creating an inclusive workplace isn't just a leadership responsibility. An inclusive workplace requires the involvement of every employee. Professionals must actively foster respect, understanding, and equal opportunities in their work environments.

1. Promoting Inclusive Collaboration and Respect

Employees should advocate for inclusivity by encouraging diverse participation, listening actively, and fostering respectful communication in group settings.

Example:

> During a weekly strategy meeting at MacTech University's DAUR office, the team was discussing outreach plans for the upcoming alumni weekend. *Ethan Park*, a seasoned, enthusiastic staff member, dominated much of

the conversation, sharing multiple ideas and speaking at length.

Noticing that others hadn't had a chance to contribute, *Alice Han*, the Assistant Director of Alumni Engagement, gently stepped in and said, "Ethan, I really appreciate your energy on this, I'd love to hear different perspectives too. *Priya*, what are your thoughts on how we might engage younger alumni?"

Her comment shifted the dynamic of the meeting. Priya Desai, a newer team member, shared a fresh idea involving social media ambassadors, which sparked a productive discussion and ultimately became part of the final plan.

By creating space for quieter voices, Alice reinforced a culture of inclusion and psychological safety. Her approach ensured that all team members felt heard and respected, leading to more balanced collaboration and stronger outcomes.

2. Supporting Employee Resource Groups (ERGs) and DEI Initiatives

Professionals can engage with workplace DEI programs, such as Employee Resource Groups (ERGs), to advocate for diversity and inclusion.

Example:

At MacTech University, *Danielle Fairchild*, a senior communications manager in the Division of Alumni and University Relations (DAUR), joined the university's "Women in Leadership" Employee Resource Group (ERG). Motivated by her own experiences navigating career advancement, Danielle wanted to support and mentor emerging female professionals across departments.

Through the ERG, she began mentoring *Mary Shelley*, a newer staff member in the Career Center, helping her build confidence, expand her network, and prepare for leadership opportunities. Danielle also collaborated with HR to organize panel discussions featuring women leaders from across the university, creating space for open dialogue and shared learning.

Her involvement not only helped individual colleagues grow but also contributed to a more inclusive and supportive workplace culture. By actively participating in DEI initiatives like the ERG, Danielle played a key role in fostering equity, visibility, and professional development for women at MacTech.

An employee joins their company's "Women in Leadership ERG" to help mentor and support female colleagues in advancing their careers. By participating in DEI initiatives, employees contribute to positive workplace change.

3. Calling Out Bias and Advocating for Fair Policies

Professionals must recognize and challenge biased workplace practices that create inequities in hiring, promotions, or team dynamics.

Example:

> At MacTech University, the Career Center was expanding its team to support new student success initiatives. During the hiring process, *Alicia Rivers*, a coordinator on the hiring committee, noticed a pattern: the committee consistently passed over candidates from underrepresented backgrounds, despite them having strong qualifications.
>
> Concerned about the potential influence of unconscious bias, Alicia raised the issue with *Mark Cliff*, the committee chair and Director of Career Services. Together, they reviewed past hiring data and found similar trends across previous searches.
>
> Rather than ignoring the issue, the team took action. They introduced structured interview rubrics, implemented blind resume reviews to remove identifying information, and provided bias awareness training for all committee members. These changes led to a more equitable and transparent process.
>
> In the next round of hiring, the candidate pool was more diverse, and the final selection included *Jamal Laurier*, a highly qualified

applicant whose resume might have previously been overlooked. His contributions later helped expand outreach to underserved student populations.

A hiring committee notices that candidates from certain backgrounds are consistently overlooked due to unconscious bias. Employees speak up and encourage structured, objective hiring processes, such as blind resume reviews, to create a fairer recruitment system.

Advocating for inclusivity ensures that workplaces value and support all employees, creating stronger teams and ethical business practices.

Recognizing and Addressing Unconscious Biases
Unconscious biases, automatic assumptions or stereotypes that affect decisions, can impact workplace relationships, hiring, and promotions without individuals realizing it. Recognizing and addressing these biases helps ensure fairness and equal opportunities for all employees.

1. Understanding the Impact of Bias in the Workplace

Unconscious bias can lead to unfair hiring decisions, limited career growth for certain groups, and workplace exclusion. Employees should identify biases and take steps to counteract them.

Example:

> At MacTech University's Division of Alumni and University Relations (DAUR), *Elena*

Shepherd, a recent graduate and new program coordinator, consistently demonstrated initiative and strong organizational skills. However, her manager, *Tom Little*, a longtime department head, unconsciously assumed that Elena wasn't ready for leadership opportunities due to her age and limited years of experience.

When a team lead position opened up for an upcoming alumni engagement project, Tom initially overlooked Elena for the role. During a one on one check-in, Elena expressed interest in taking on more responsibility and shared examples of how she had successfully led smaller initiatives.

This prompted Tom to reflect on his assumptions. Realizing the oversight, he enrolled Elena in a leadership development workshop offered by HR and paired her with *Danielle*, a senior staff member, for mentorship. Elena later co-led the alumni project with great success, earning praise from colleagues and senior leadership.

By recognizing and addressing his bias, Tom ensured that professional development opportunities were based on potential and performance, not age. This not only supported Elena's growth but also reinforced a culture of equity and inclusion within the department.

A manager assumes that a younger employee lacks leadership skills due to their age. This bias prevents the employee from receiving growth opportunities. By addressing this assumption, the manager provides training and mentorship, ensuring fair professional development.

2. Using Bias Reduction Strategies

Employees can reduce unconscious bias by embracing diverse perspectives, questioning assumptions, and implementing fair decision making processes.

Example:

> At MacTech University, *Rose Sinclair*, the Associate Director of Alumni Relations, was leading a search for a new engagement coordinator. After reviewing the final round of candidates, she found herself leaning toward *Lisa Knight*, whose background and communication style felt familiar and comfortable, similar to Rose's own early career path.
>
> However, during a follow up discussion with *Malik Hawes*, a colleague from HR and a member of the hiring committee, Rose reflected on her preference and realized it was influenced more by personal similarity than by objective qualifications. Malik encouraged her to revisit the evaluation rubric and compare candidates based solely on skills, experience, and interview performance.

Upon doing so, Rose recognized that *Jamal Laurier*, another finalist, had stronger experience in digital engagement and had led successful alumni campaigns at his previous institution. Refocusing on the criteria, Rose and the committee selected Jamal for the role.

By questioning her instincts, Rose helped ensure the hiring process was equitable and merit based. This example illustrates how self-awareness and structured evaluation can reduce bias and lead to better, more inclusive hiring decisions.

A hiring manager questions her own instincts when preferring one candidate over another based on personal similarity rather than qualifications. By refocusing on objective criteria, she selects the most qualified candidate rather than allowing bias to influence hiring.

Best Practices:

- Attend DEI training to recognize bias in workplace decision making.
- Seek diverse viewpoints before making assumptions.
- Encourage fair hiring and promotion policies in team discussions.

Final Flex
Employers expect professionals to embrace inclusivity, as DEI enhances collaboration, innovation, and workplace satisfaction. Employees should advocate for

inclusivity, challenge unconscious bias, and contribute to an equitable professional environment where everyone has opportunities to grow and thrive.

DEI is more than just a corporate initiative, it's a workplace necessity that benefits both employees and businesses. Companies that prioritize diversity and inclusion build stronger teams, encourage innovation, and create positive workplace cultures for long term success.

Chapter 9: Technology: Navigating the Digital Age

In today's digital first workplace, technology is more than a tool, it's a career catalyst. This chapter explores how mastering digital literacy, technical skills, and cybersecurity awareness positions young professionals for success across industries. From leveraging data analytics and cloud collaboration to embracing artificial intelligence for automation and strategic insights, the ability to adapt to emerging technologies is no longer optional, it's essential. Through practical examples and actionable strategies, this chapter equips readers to integrate technology into their workflows, enhance productivity, and build a competitive edge in a rapidly evolving job market.

Technology plays a critical role in every industry. Employers expect professionals to embrace digital tools, stay updated on emerging trends, and apply technical skills to streamline productivity.

Why Employers Expect Young Employees to Embrace Digital Tools and Technical Skills
In today's technology driven workplace, digital literacy and technical skills are no longer optional, they are essential for career success. Employers look for young professionals who are familiar with digital tools and apply them strategically to enhance productivity, streamline workflows, and solve complex problems. Staying updated on emerging trends, maintaining cybersecurity awareness, and leveraging artificial

intelligence (AI) for efficiency and innovation significantly increase a candidate's value in any industry.

Must-Have Technical Skills for Different Career Paths
Different industries require distinct technical competencies. However, establishing a foundation in digital tools, data analysis, and technology integration is universally beneficial. Below are key technical skills employers expect across various career paths:

1. Business and Administration

    ➥ Data Analytics & Excel Proficiency: Ability to analyze business trends, track financial data, and generate reports.

    ➥ CRM Software Knowledge: Familiarity with Salesforce, HubSpot, or other customer management platforms.

    ➥ Project Management Tools: Understanding of Asana, Trello, or Monday.com for organizing workflows.

Example:

> At MacTech University, *Nina Bajaj*, a senior business analyst in the Office of Finance and Budget, was tasked with helping university leadership understand the financial impact of expanding student success initiatives, including RamConnect.

The raw data, spanning enrollment trends, alumni donations, and departmental spending, was complex and difficult to interpret in spreadsheet form. To make the information more accessible, Nina used Power BI to create interactive dashboards that visualized key metrics, including cost-benefit analyses, projected ROI, and funding gaps.

During a presentation to *Dr. Laura Sullivan*, the Vice President for Academic Affairs, Nina walked through the dashboards, allowing leadership to explore different scenarios and parse specific data points. The visual clarity helped the team quickly identify areas of concern and confidently approve a phased funding plan.

By translating complex financial data into actionable insights, Nina's use of data visualization tools improved decision making and demonstrated the strategic value of analytics in higher education.

2. Marketing and Communications

➡ SEO & Digital Advertising: Understanding Google Analytics, keyword research, and online ad campaigns.

➡ Social Media Management: Knowledge of scheduling tools like Hootsuite or Buffer.

➥ Content Creation & Editing: Ability to use Canva, Adobe Creative Suite, or video editing software.

Example:

> At MacTech University, *Luis Hernandez*, a marketing coordinator in the Division of Alumni and University Relations (DAUR), managed the university's alumni blog. While his content was strong, website traffic had plateaued, and engagement metrics were lower than expected.
>
> To address this, Luis began using SEO tools like SEMrush and Google Search Console to analyze keyword performance, backlink opportunities, and page load times. He also used Yoast SEO within the blog's CMS to optimize headlines, meta descriptions, and readability scores.
>
> One of his key insights was that alumni were frequently searching for career related content. Luis collaborated with the Career Center to publish a series of blog posts on networking, mentoring, and job search strategies, each optimized with targeted keywords and internal links to RamConnect.
>
> Within three months, blog traffic increased by 40%, and alumni engagement on related platforms saw a noticeable uptick. By leveraging SEO tools strategically, Luis helped MacTech improve its digital reach and deepen connections with its alumni community.

3. IT and Software Development

➡ Coding & Programming: Proficiency in Python, JavaScript, C++, or SQL.

➡ Cloud Computing & Networking: Understanding AWS, Azure, and database management.

➡ Cybersecurity Fundamentals: Ability to assess vulnerabilities and implement security protocols.

Example:

At MacTech University, *Gary Leonard*, a software engineer in the IT Services department, developed a secure web portal for alumni to access personalized career resources through RamConnect. The portal needed to handle sensitive data, including employment history, mentoring interactions, and contact information.

To ensure both efficiency and data protection, Gary Leonard built the application using Microsoft Azure, integrating cloud native security features such as identity management, role based access control, and encrypted data storage. He also used Azure App Services to streamline deployment and scalability, allowing the portal to handle increased traffic during peak alumni engagement periods.

Gary Leonard collaborated with *Nina Bajaj*, a business analyst, to visualize usage metrics and identify areas for performance optimization. Thanks to Azure's cloud based architecture, updates were rolled out seamlessly, and the system maintained high availability and compliance with university data policies.

By leveraging secure cloud solutions, Gary Leonard ensured the application was both robust and scalable, supporting MacTech's mission to connect alumni and students while safeguarding their data.

4. Healthcare and Life Sciences

➥ Electronic Health Records (EHR) Systems: Knowledge of Epic or Cerner software.

➥ Telemedicine Platforms: Ability to facilitate remote patient care through secure networks.

➥ Medical Research Tools: Familiarity with AI driven diagnostics and biotechnology software.

Example:

At MacTech Medical Group, *Erika Ramstein*, a nurse practitioner specializing in family medicine, noticed that many of her patients were missing follow up appointments. After looking through their files, she discovered that a majority of those patients lived in the Bronx, and struggled with mobility challenges or demanding work schedules,

To address this, Erica began using telehealth software, integrated with the clinic's electronic health record system, to conduct virtual consultations. Through platforms like Epic Telehealth and Zoom for Healthcare, she could check in with patients remotely, manage chronic conditions, and provide timely care without requiring in person visits.

One patient, *Mr. Jorge Alvarez*, a single father working two jobs, had been struggling to manage his diabetes due to missed appointments. With virtual visits, Erika could monitor his progress, adjust medications, and offer nutritional guidance, all from the convenience of his home.

By embracing telehealth, Erika increased patient accessibility, reduced no show rates, and improved health outcomes, demonstrating how technology can bridge gaps in care and support community health.

Cybersecurity Basics for Workplace Safety
Cybersecurity awareness is critical for protecting company data, personal information, and preventing cyber threats. Employers expect employees to understand risks, follow security protocols, and recognize potential threats.

1. Password Protection and Multi-Factor Authentication (MFA)

Employees must use strong passwords and MFA authentication to safeguard company accounts.

Example:

> A finance department implements MFA for sensitive transactions, ensuring unauthorized users cannot access critical data.

2. Recognizing Phishing Attacks

Phishing scams deceive employees into sharing sensitive information or clicking harmful links. Recognizing suspicious emails prevents security breaches.

Example:

> A new employee receives an email requesting bank details. Instead of responding, they verify with IT and avoid compromising company security.

3. Securing Devices and Networks

Using encrypted connections, VPNs, and updating software protects against cyberattacks.

Example:

> A remote worker ensures their home Wi-Fi is secured and avoids using public networks for company logins, reducing cybersecurity vulnerabilities.

Using Digital Tools Effectively to Maximize Efficiency
Employers value professionals who understand digital tools and apply them to optimize productivity. Smart use of workplace technology improves organization, reduces repetitive tasks, and accelerates results.

1. Automation for Workflow Optimization

Employees can automate repetitive tasks to increase efficiency and reduce errors.

Example:

> At MacTech University, *Tasha Greene*, an HR specialist in the Office of Human Resources, noticed that the manual onboarding process for new hires was time consuming and inconsistent. Each department had its own approach, and important information, like benefits enrollment, IT setup, and orientation schedules, was sometimes delayed or missed.

> To improve the experience, Tasha implemented an automated onboarding workflow using Microsoft Outlook and Power Automate. She created a series of scheduled emails that welcomed new employees, introduced them to key contacts, and provided step by step guidance for their first week. The emails included links to training modules, policy documents, and a personalized checklist based on the employee's role.

One new hire, *Luis Hernandez*, a marketing coordinator in DAUR, shared that the automated emails helped him feel prepared and supported from day one. He was able to complete all required tasks on time and quickly integrate into his team.

By setting up automated onboarding communications, Tasha saved time for HR staff, reduced errors, and ensured a smoother, more consistent experience for new employees, demonstrating how thoughtful use of technology can enhance workplace efficiency and engagement.

2. Cloud Collaboration for Remote Work

Using Google Drive, Microsoft Teams, and Slack enables seamless remote collaboration.

Example:

> At MacTech University, *Mei Ru Liu*, a graphic designer in the Division of Alumni and University Relations (DAUR), was working on a series of digital assets for the upcoming alumni weekend campaign. The project required close coordination with *Luis Hernandez*, the marketing coordinator, and *Danielle Fairchild*, the communications manager.
>
> To streamline collaboration and avoid delays caused by email attachments and version confusion, Mei set up shared folders using Microsoft OneDrive and Adobe Creative Cloud

Libraries. These platforms allowed the team to access design files in real time, leave comments directly on drafts, and track updates without needing to request the latest version.

When Luis needed to quickly revise a social media graphic, he simply left a note in the shared folder. Mei was able to make the change within the hour, and Danielle could then review and approve the final version without scheduling a separate meeting.

Using shared cloud folders, Mei reduced communication delays, improved workflow efficiency, and ensured that the team stayed aligned, demonstrating how digital tools can enhance creative collaboration in a fast paced environment.

3. Data Management for Smarter Decision Making

Businesses rely on data collection and analytics to guide strategy. Employees who use Excel formulas, AI powered analytics, and reporting dashboards are highly valuable.

Example:

At a MacTech University bookstore managed by *Alice Han*, a retail operations manager, sales of merchandise, especially apparel and tech accessories, varied widely depending on the time of year, campus events, and student trends. Intuition and past experiences often decided inventory, which sometimes led to overstocking or missed opportunities.

To improve accuracy, Alice began using AI driven analytics tools like Microsoft Dynamics 365 Retail Insights to analyze customer purchasing patterns. The system processed point of sale data, seasonal trends, and even social media engagement to forecast demand more precisely.

The tool revealed that RamConnect branded hoodies saw a spike in sales during mentoring events and orientation week. Based on this insight, Alice adjusted inventory levels ahead of the fall semester, ensuring popular items were well stocked while reducing excess in slower moving categories.

As a result, the store saw a 25% increase in apparel sales and a noticeable reduction in unsold inventory. By leveraging AI tools, Alice made data informed decisions that improved operational efficiency and enhanced the customer experience.

How Embracing Artificial Intelligence (AI) Can Make Employees More Valuable
AI is revolutionizing workplace efficiency, and employees who understand the technology position themselves as future leaders. AI can assist with automation, predictive analytics, and smart decision making, making professionals indispensable.

1. AI for Productivity Enhancement

AI automates tasks such as email sorting, appointment scheduling, and customer inquiries, freeing up time for strategic work.

Example:

> At Salesforce's New York regional office, *Avery Samuels*, a senior sales executive, managed a large portfolio of prospective clients in the higher education sector. With dozens of leads coming in weekly, it became difficult to prioritize follow ups and identify which prospects were most likely to convert.
>
> To streamline his workflow, Avery began using Salesforce Einstein, the company's AI powered CRM tool. The system analyzed historical data, engagement patterns, and lead behavior to score prospects based on conversion likelihood. It also flagged high priority leads and suggested optimal times for outreach.
>
> One lead, *MacTech University*, interacted with several product demos but hadn't yet committed. Einstein flagged the account as high potential, prompting Avery to schedule a personalized follow up. Within two weeks, MacTech signed a multi-year contract to implement Salesforce tools across its alumni engagement and student success platforms.
>
> By leveraging AI powered CRM software, Avery ensured timely follow ups, improved lead

prioritization, and increased his conversion rate, demonstrating how smart technology can drive strategic sales success.

2. AI in Data Analysis and Reporting

Companies use AI to analyze massive datasets and generate insights faster than manual calculations.

Example:

> At Morgan Stanley's Midtown Manhattan office, *Nicole Lennox*, a financial analyst specializing in technology sector investments, was tasked with advising institutional clients on portfolio strategy. With market volatility increasing, Nicole needed more precise forecasting tools to guide decision making.
>
> She began using AI driven platforms like Kensho and Bloomberg Terminal's machine learning models to analyze historical stock performance, news sentiment, and macroeconomic indicators. With their findings, she could successfully identify patterns and predict short term trends in high growth tech stocks.
>
> For example, the AI models flagged a likely upward movement in *Nvidia's* stock based on increased demand for AI chips and positive earnings sentiment. Using this insight, Nicole recommended a timely buy to her clients, who saw strong returns within the quarter.

By integrating AI powered forecasting into her workflow, Nicole improved the accuracy of her predictions, enhanced client trust, and demonstrated how technology can elevate financial strategy in a competitive market.

3. AI for Personalization and Customer Engagement

AI helps businesses create personalized experiences, improving user satisfaction and retention.

Example:

At *Urban Threads*, a growing online apparel retailer based in New Jersey, *Alicia Rivers*, the e-commerce specialist, noticed that many customers were abandoning their carts or leaving the site without getting answers to basic questions like sizing, shipping times, or return policies.

To improve the customer experience and reduce lost sales, Alicia integrated an AI powered chatbot using Zendesk AI and Shopify's chatbot plugin. The chatbot was trained to handle common inquiries 24/7, provide personalized product recommendations, and even offer discount codes to hesitant shoppers.

One weekend, during a flash sale, the chatbot handled over 1,200 customer interactions, resolving 85% of them without needing human intervention. It helped one customer select the right size of a limited edition hoodie, and guided another through the checkout process after she had trouble applying a promotion.

As a result, Urban Threads saw a 30% increase in completed purchases during the sale and a noticeable drop in customer service response times. Alicia's strategic use of AI not only improved efficiency but also directly contributed to higher customer satisfaction and increased revenue.

Why Young Professionals Must Embrace AI

- Stay ahead of competition - AI is shaping industries, and early adopters gain an advantage in the job market.
- Boost productivity - AI automates mundane tasks, allowing professionals to focus on strategy and creativity.
- Improve decision-making - AI assists in data interpretation, forecasting, and optimizing workflows.

Artificial intelligence is no longer a distant concept reserved for tech giants and computer scientists. It's a transformative force reshaping every industry. For young professionals, regardless of discipline, embracing AI early in their college journey is not just a strategic advantage, it's a necessity.

AI is the new literacy. Just as previous generations had to master digital tools and internet fluency, today's students must understand how AI works, where it's headed, and how it can be ethically and effectively applied in their field. Whether you're a future educator using AI to personalize learning, a business major optimizing operations with predictive analytics, or a communications student leveraging AI for audience insights, the possibilities are endless and growing.

Starting early allows students to build confidence. Experimenting with tools like ChatGPT, Tableau, or machine learning platforms, and asking critical questions about bias, transparency, and impact are beneficial. Learning AI proactively also opens doors to internships, research opportunities, and leadership roles in shaping how AI is used responsibly.

Diving into certifications that talk about AI basics and machine learning are equally important. Understand the technology itself and not just the tools. Look at Salesforce Trailhead, Microsoft Azure, and IBM SkillsBuild AI Experiential Learning Lab.

Most importantly, embracing AI is about empowerment, and ensuring that young professionals are not just passive users of technology, but active contributors to its development and direction. Learning to harness AI thoughtfully and creatively affords students access to leadership positions in a future that demands both innovation and integrity.

Final Flex
Employers expect young professionals to embrace digital literacy, they particularly seek individuals who demonstrate strong cybersecurity awareness, proficiency in digital collaboration, and knowledge of

AI powered automation. Professionals who continuously adapt to technology trends, refine their technical competencies, and integrate AI into their workflows set job candidates apart, and become indispensable assets to companies, ensuring long term career growth and success.

Chapter 10: AI as Your Career Accelerator

Artificial intelligence is no longer a futuristic concept; it's a career accelerator that defines success in today's marketplace. This chapter explores how AI can amplify human potential, transforming professionals from task executors into strategic thinkers. It covers practical applications such as prompt engineering for job search and interview preparation, AI powered resume optimization, skill gap analysis, and continuous learning strategies.

Artificial intelligence has become an essential career tool in the contemporary marketplace. Young professionals who master AI applications don't just gain a competitive edge, they position themselves as forward thinking leaders, ready to drive innovation in any industry. This chapter explores how to harness AI strategically throughout your career journey, from landing your first job to continuous professional development.

The AI Advantage: Why It Matters for Your Career
Artificial intelligence is revolutionizing nearly every aspect of life, across industries, and AI literacy has become as fundamental as computer skills were in the 1990s.

The professionals who thrive in the coming decades won't be those who fear AI replacement, but those who understand how AI tools amplify their human capabilities. Learning to work alongside AI will transform you from a job seeker into a problem solver, from a task executor into a strategic thinker.

Consider this: companies are increasingly looking for employees who can bridge the gap between human creativity and AI efficiency. When you demonstrate AI fluency during interviews, you signal that you're not just ready for today's workplace; you're prepared to help shape tomorrow's.

Mastering Prompt Engineering for Career Development

Prompt engineering, or how to effectively communicate with AI systems, has emerged as one of the most valuable professional competencies. Think of it as learning a new language that unlocks unprecedented productivity and creativity.

The Foundation of Effective Prompts

Successful prompt engineering follows key principles that mirror effective human communication: clarity, context, and specificity. When working with AI tools like ChatGPT, Claude, or industry specific platforms, your results improve dramatically when you provide clear instructions, relevant background information, and specific desired outcomes.

Example of Basic vs. Advanced Prompting:

> *Basic:* "Help me write a resume."

> *Advanced:* "I'm a marketing major graduating in May 2025, applying for digital marketing

coordinator positions at mid-size technology companies. I have internship experience at a nonprofit, strong social media skills, and coursework in analytics. Please help me craft a resume that highlights my data driven approach to marketing and positions me as someone who can contribute immediately to growth focused teams."

The advanced prompt provides context, specificity, and clear objectives, resulting in dramatically more useful output.

Career-Specific Prompt Templates
Job Search Prompts:

- "Analyze this job posting for [position] and identify the top 5 skills and qualifications emphasized. Then suggest how I can highlight relevant experiences from my background in [field/major]."

- "Based on my resume, what are potential red flags employers might see, and how can I proactively address them in my cover letter?"

Interview Preparation Prompts:

- "I'm interviewing for [specific role] at [company type]. Based on current industry trends, what are 3 strategic questions I should ask to demonstrate my understanding of their challenges?"

- "Help me prepare STAR method responses for behavioral questions related to leadership, problem solving, and teamwork, using examples from my experience in [specific context]."

Professional Development Prompts:

- "I want to transition from [current field] to [target field] within 18 months. Create a learning roadmap that identifies skill gaps, suggests resources, and provides monthly milestones."

- "Analyze emerging trends in [industry] and recommend 3 skills I should develop to stay competitive over the next 5 years."

AI Tools for Resume Writing and Optimization
Your resume is often your first impression with potential employers, and AI can help you create documents that not only pass applicant tracking systems (ATS) but also compel human reviewers to take action.

Resume Enhancement with AI
Modern AI tools can analyze job descriptions, identify key requirements, and help you optimize your resume for maximum impact. However, the key is using AI as a collaborative partner, not a replacement for your authentic experiences and voice.

Strategic AI Resume Applications:

1. Keyword Optimization: Upload job descriptions to AI tools to identify industry specific keywords and phrases that should appear naturally in your resume.

2. Impact Quantification: AI can help you transform basic job duties into achievement focused bullet points. For example, turning "Managed social media accounts" into "Increased social media engagement by 40% across 3 platforms, reaching 15,000+ monthly users through strategic content planning and community interaction."

3. Format Optimization: AI can suggest formatting improvements that enhance readability and ATS compatibility while maintaining professional appearance.

4. Industry Customization: Different industries have distinct resume conventions. AI can help you adapt your core experiences to match expectations in finance, tech, healthcare, education, or other fields.

Example:

Sarah Chen, a business major interested in sustainability consulting, used AI to transform her basic internship experience into compelling resume content:

Original: "Intern at local environmental nonprofit. Helped with various projects."

AI-Enhanced: "Environmental Policy Research Intern | Green Future Alliance

- Conducted market analysis of renewable energy adoption trends, contributing to policy recommendations presented to city council

- Collaborated with 5 person research team to develop sustainability assessment framework, improving client evaluation efficiency by 25%

- Created data visualizations using Excel and Tableau, transforming complex environmental data into accessible reports for community stakeholders"

The AI helped Sarah recognize the strategic value of her experiences and articulate them in language that resonates with consulting firms.

AI-Powered Interview Preparation
Interview anxiety often stems from uncertainty about what to expect and how to respond effectively. AI tools can help you prepare by simulating various interview scenarios and providing personalized feedback.

Mock Interview Practice with AI
AI interview platforms can conduct realistic practice sessions, ask follow up questions based on your responses, and provide detailed feedback on your

answers, body language (through video analysis), and overall presentation.

Key AI Interview Prep Strategies:

1. Behavioral Question Banking: AI can generate dozens of behavioral questions specific to your target role and industry, helping you practice STAR method responses until they become natural.

2. Company Research Intelligence: AI can analyze a company's recent news, financial reports, and industry position to help you ask informed questions and demonstrate genuine interest.

3. Technical Skill Assessment: For roles requiring specific technical knowledge, AI can create customized quizzes and scenarios that test your abilities and identify areas for improvement.

4. Communication Pattern Analysis: Advanced AI tools can analyze your speaking patterns, identifying filler words, pacing issues, or unclear explanations that might undermine your interview performance.

Industry Specific Interview Prep

- Technology Sector: AI can offer practice coding challenges, system design questions, nd technical explanations that make complex concepts accessible to non-technical stakeholders.

- Healthcare and Life Sciences: Practice ethical scenarios, patient case discussions, and regulatory knowledge questions that demonstrate both technical competency and humanistic values.
- Business and Finance: Prepare for case study analyses, market trend discussions, and quantitative problem solving scenarios that showcase analytical thinking.
- Education and Nonprofits: Develop responses that demonstrate passion for mission driven work while highlighting measurable impacts and collaborative achievements.

Using AI for Skill Gap Analysis

One of AI's most powerful career applications identifies and helps users bridge skill gaps before they become obstacles. By analyzing job market trends, required competencies, and your current abilities, AI can create personalized development roadmaps.

Comprehensive Skill Assessment

AI tools can evaluate your resume, LinkedIn profile, portfolio, and career goals to provide objective assessments of your professional strengths and development opportunities.

AI-Driven Skill Analysis Process:

1. Current State Assessment: AI analyzes your educational background, work experience,

certifications, and demonstrated competencies to create a comprehensive skill inventory.

2. Market Demand Analysis: AI processes thousands of job postings in your target field, identifying the most in-demand skills, both hard and soft.

3. Gap Identification: AI compares your abilities with market demands, highlighting specific areas where additional development would improve your competitiveness.

4. Learning Path Optimization: Based on your learning style, time availability, and career timeline, AI suggests the most efficient sequence for acquiring new skills.

Example: Marketing Professional Skill Gap Analysis

Alex Myers, a recent graduate with a marketing degree, used AI to analyze the digital marketing job market:

AI Analysis Results:

- Strong Areas: Content creation, social media management, brand awareness

- Skill Gaps: Marketing automation (HubSpot/Marketo), Google Analytics certification, SQL for marketing data analysis, A/B testing methodology

- Recommended Timeline: 6 month intensive development plan

- Priority Sequence: Google Analytics certification (Month 1) → Marketing automation platform training (Months 2-3) → Basic SQL for marketers (Months 4-5) → A/B testing certification (Month 6)

This analysis helped Alex focus development efforts on high-impact skills that directly addressed employer needs rather than pursuing generic professional development.

Staying Relevant as AI Evolves
The AI landscape changes rapidly, with new tools, capabilities, and applications regularly emerging. Professionals who build systems for continuous AI learning will remain valuable regardless of how technology evolves.

Building an AI Learning Ecosystem
Stay Connected to AI Developments:

➥ Subscribe to AI newsletters and research publications

➥ Join professional communities focused on AI applications in your industry

➥ Attend webinars and conferences that explore AI's practical business applications

➡ Follow thought leaders who bridge AI technology with real world implementation

Hands On Experimentation:

➡ Regularly test new AI tools and platforms relevant to your field

➡ Participate in AI hackathons or innovation challenges

➡ Create personal projects that explore AI applications in your area of interest

➡ Document your experiences and share insights with your professional network

The Human AI Collaboration Mindset

The future belongs to professionals who see AI as a powerful collaborator rather than a threat or replacement. This requires developing what experts call "AI partnership thinking"; the ability to identify where human creativity, emotional intelligence, and strategic thinking combine most effectively with AI's analytical and processing capabilities.

Key Collaboration Principles:

1. AI Handles Data, Humans Provide Context: Let AI process information and identify patterns, while you provide strategic interpretation and decision making.

2. AI Suggests, Humans Judge: Use AI generated options and recommendations as starting points for your professional judgment and expertise.

3. AI Automates, Humans Innovate: Allow AI to handle routine tasks so you can focus on creative problem-solving and relationship building.

4. AI Scales, Humans Personalize: Leverage AI's ability to handle large volumes while you provide the personal touch that builds trust and understanding.

Advanced AI Applications for Career Growth
As you become comfortable with basic AI applications, more sophisticated engagement can accelerate your career development and professional impact.

AI for Professional Networking
AI can transform how you network by helping you identify valuable connections, craft personalized outreach messages, and maintain meaningful professional relationships at scale.

Strategic Networking with AI:

- Analyze LinkedIn networks to identify mutual connections and warm introduction opportunities
- Generate personalized outreach messages that reference shared interests, experiences, or professional challenges
- Track relationship development and suggest appropriate follow up timing and content

- Identify networking events and professional communities where you're likely to meet valuable contacts

AI for Thought Leadership Development
Building a professional reputation as a thoughtful industry contributor requires consistent, valuable content creation. AI can help you develop and maintain thought leadership presence without overwhelming your schedule.

Content Strategy with AI Support:

- Analyze trending topics in your industry and suggest unique angles for your expertise

- Generate content outlines and first drafts that you can refine with your personal insights

- Optimize content for different platforms (LinkedIn articles, Twitter threads, blog posts, conference presentations)

- Track engagement patterns to understand what resonates with your professional audience

AI for Career Decision Making
Major career decisions, job offers, career pivots, geographic moves, benefit from comprehensive analyses that consider multiple variables and long term implications. AI can help you evaluate options more objectively.

Decision Support Applications:

- Analyze job offers holistically, considering salary, benefits, growth potential, company culture, and industry trends

- Model different career path scenarios and their likely outcomes over 5-10 year timeframes

- Evaluate geographic markets for opportunities, cost of living, and professional community strength

- Assess educational investment decisions (graduate school, certifications, bootcamps) based on ROI and career impact

Ethical AI Use in Professional Development
As AI becomes integral to career development, understanding ethical use principles ensures you maintain authenticity while leveraging these powerful tools responsibly.

Authenticity in AI Assisted Applications
While AI can significantly improve your job search materials and interview preparation, the goal is to enhance, not replace, your authentic self. AI should help you communicate your experiences, values, and perspective more effectively, not create fictional narratives.

Ethical Guidelines:

- Use AI to improve your rhetoric, not to create false stories

- Always fact check and verify AI generated content before using it professionally

- Maintain transparency about AI assistance when appropriate (e.g., in academic or research contexts)

- Respect intellectual property and plagiarism guidelines in your industry

Privacy and Data Security

Professional AI tool use requires careful attention to data privacy, especially when inputting sensitive information like resumes, salary details, or company specific information.

Best Practices:

- Read privacy policies and understand how AI platforms handle your data

- Avoid inputting confidential company information into public AI tools

- Use generic examples when possible during AI interaction

- Regularly review and delete personal data from AI platforms when no longer needed

Measuring AI's Impact on Your Career
To ensure your AI investment pays dividends, establish metrics that track how AI usage translates into career advancement and professional growth.

Job Search Effectiveness:

- Time from application to interview invitation
- Interview to offer conversion rate
- Quality of opportunities and salary progression
- Network growth and engagement rates

Professional Development:

- Skill acquisition speed and retention
- Project completion efficiency
- Recognition and feedback quality
- Leadership opportunity frequency

Long term Career Trajectory:

- Promotion timeline and scope of responsibilities
- Industry reputation and thought leadership metrics
- Professional satisfaction and work-life balance
- Financial and career goal achievement

The Future Ready Professional
As AI continues evolving, the professionals who maintain curiosity, adaptability, and commitment to continuous learning will thrive. By building strong AI

collaboration skills now, you're not just preparing for your next job, you're developing capabilities that will serve your entire career.

The key insight this chapter offers is that AI amplifies human potential rather than replacing it. Your creativity, emotional intelligence, ethical reasoning, and relationship building abilities become more valuable, not less, when combined with AI's analytical and processing power.

Start experimenting with AI tools today. Begin with simple applications like resume optimization or interview practice, then gradually expand to more sophisticated uses like skill gap analysis and strategic career planning. The professionals who begin this journey now will lead the industries of tomorrow.

Remember: AI is not about becoming more machine like in your approach to career development. It's also not about short cuts! It's about becoming more strategically human, using technology to handle routine analysis so you can focus on the uniquely human work of building meaningful careers that create value for yourself, your employers, and society.

Chapter 11: Digital Fluency Essentials

This chapter explores the concept of digital fluency as a critical competency for modern professionals. It moves beyond basic computer literacy to emphasize strategic use of technology for problem solving, workflow optimization, and career advancement. Key areas include mastering cloud collaboration tools for seamless remote teamwork, applying data visualization principles to make information actionable, and developing foundational coding skills to enhance automation and communication with technical teams. By integrating these capabilities, professionals can adapt to evolving technologies and create meaningful impact across diverse industries.

Digital fluency extends far beyond basic computer skills. Contemporary workplaces require professionals to navigate cloud environments, interpret data visually, understand fundamental coding concepts, and maintain security in remote work settings. This chapter provides practical frameworks for developing these essential digital competencies, regardless of your primary field of study or career focus.

Redefining Digital Fluency for the Modern Workplace
Digital fluency encompasses the ability to effectively evaluate, use, and create digital tools and systems to accomplish professional goals. Unlike digital literacy, which focuses on basic usage, digital fluency requires strategic thinking about how technology can solve

problems, streamline workflows, and create competitive advantages.

Modern digital fluency involves three core dimensions:

- Technical Proficiency: Understanding how digital tools work and how to use them effectively

- Strategic Application: Knowing when and why to use specific tools for maximum impact

- Adaptive Learning: Continuously updating skills as technology evolves

For young professionals, digital fluency serves as a career accelerator across all industries. Whether you're entering healthcare, education, finance, manufacturing, or creative fields, employers expect you to bring technological solutions to traditional challenges.

Cloud Collaboration Mastery: Working Seamlessly Across Distance and Time
Cloud collaboration has transformed from a convenience into a necessity. The professionals who excel at virtual teamwork, document sharing, and remote project management gain significant advantages in flexibility, productivity, and career opportunities.

Modern cloud collaboration involves multiple interconnected platforms working together to support different aspects of teamwork. Rather than mastering individual tools in isolation, digital fluency requires understanding how these systems integrate and complement each other.

Core Cloud Collaboration Components:

File Storage and Sharing: Google Drive, Microsoft OneDrive, Dropbox Business Communication Platforms: Slack, Microsoft Teams, Discord (for creative industries)

Project Management: Asana, Monday.com, Trello, Notion

Document Creation: Google Workspace, Microsoft 365, collaborative tools like Figma for design

Video Conferencing: Zoom, Google Meet, Microsoft Teams integrated calling

Advanced Cloud Collaboration Strategies
Version Control and Document Management: Effective cloud collaboration requires systematic approaches to document versioning, permission management, and file organization. Poor document management creates confusion, duplicated work, and missed deadlines.

Best Practices:

- Establish clear naming conventions that include dates, version numbers, and contributor initials

- Use folder hierarchies that make sense to all team members, not just the creator

- Set appropriate sharing permissions (view, comment, edit) based on roles and project phases

- Create master documents that serve as project dashboards, linking to all relevant files and resources

Real Time Collaboration Techniques: Modern cloud tools enable simultaneous multi-user editing, but effective real time collaboration requires coordination and communication protocols.

Strategies for Effective Real Time Work:
- Use commenting systems to discuss changes without cluttering the main document

- Establish "editing windows" where team members take turns making major revisions

- Leverage suggestion modes that allow reviewers to propose changes without directly altering content

- Create shared task lists within documents to track who's responsible for specific sections or edits

Industry Specific Cloud Collaboration Applications
Marketing and Creative Teams: Creative professionals need cloud solutions that handle large files, support visual feedback, and integrate with design software.

Example:

> *Cole Cooper*, a digital marketing coordinator at a nonprofit, managed a rebranding project involving graphic designers, copywriters, and program directors across three time zones. He used Adobe Creative Cloud for file sharing, Slack for quick communications, and Monday.com for project tracking. By creating shared brand asset libraries and establishing weekly virtual check ins, the team completed the rebrand 20% faster than similar previous projects.

Business and Analytics Teams: Business professionals require cloud solutions that support data analysis, financial modeling, and strategic planning.

Example:

> *David Lin*, a business analyst at a consulting firm, led quarterly strategic planning sessions using Microsoft Teams integrated with Power BI dashboards. Team members could access real-time data visualizations during virtual meetings, annotate shared documents simultaneously, and create action items that automatically synced with individual task lists. This approach reduced planning time by 30% while improving follow-through on strategic initiatives.

Healthcare and Research Teams: Healthcare professionals need cloud collaboration that maintains privacy compliance while supporting clinical coordination and research activities.

Example:

> *Dr. Sarah Chen*, a resident physician, used HIPAA compliant cloud platforms to coordinate patient care rounds across multiple hospital departments. Secure messaging systems allowed real-time consultation with specialists, shared digital whiteboards supported treatment planning discussions, and integrated scheduling tools helped coordinate complex care team meetings. These digital collaboration tools improved patient care continuity while reducing communication delays.

Remote Work Optimization Through Cloud Tools
Cloud collaboration excellence requires understanding how to maintain productivity, team cohesion, and professional development in remote work environments.

Creating Virtual Presence: Successful remote workers develop strong a virtual presence, including the ability to communicate effectively, contribute meaningfully, and build relationships through digital platforms.

Techniques for Strong Virtual Presence:

1. Use video strategically (on for important discussions, off for routine updates)

2. Develop clear, concise written communication that conveys tone and intent

3. Proactively share updates on project progress and availability

4. Create virtual "office hours" when colleagues know they can reach you easily

5. Participate actively in virtual team building and informal communication channels

Asynchronous Collaboration Excellence: Not all collaboration happens in real time. Professionals who excel at asynchronous work, contributing meaningfully to projects across time zones and schedules, become invaluable team members.

Asynchronous Work Strategies:

1. Record video summaries of complex ideas or project updates for team members in different time zones

2. Use collaborative documents to continue conversations between meetings

3. Create detailed handoff documentation when passing projects between team members

4. Establish clear response time expectations for different types of communication

5. Use project management tools to track dependencies and notify relevant team members of completed tasks

Data Visualization for Non-Analysts: Making Information Accessible and Actionable

Data visualization has become essential across all professional roles. You don't need to be a data scientist to effectively present information, identify trends, and support decision making through visual communication.

Visual Communication Principles

Effective data visualization follows design principles that make information clear, accurate, and compelling. Understanding these principles allows professionals in any field to create visualizations that inform and persuade.

Core Visualization Design Principles:

- Clarity Over Complexity: Choose simple, clean designs that highlight key insights rather than overwhelming viewers with excessive detail.
- Audience Appropriate Detail: Adjust complexity and technical language based on your audience's familiarity with the subject matter.
- Honest Representation: Ensure your visualizations accurately represent the underlying data without misleading or manipulating viewer interpretation.

- Strategic Color Use: Use color purposefully to highlight important information, group related data, or create visual hierarchy.
- Progressive Disclosure: Present information in layers, allowing viewers to understand high level patterns before diving into detailed analysis.

Practical Data Visualization Tools

Excel and Google Sheets Advanced Features: Most professionals already have access to spreadsheet software, but few leverage advanced visualization capabilities.

Advanced Spreadsheet Visualization Techniques:

- Create dynamic charts that update automatically as data changes

- Use conditional formatting to highlight trends and outliers

- Build interactive dashboards using pivot tables and slicers

- Design small series of similar charts that enable easy comparison across categories

- Implement data validation and dropdown menus to create user friendly data entry forms

Tableau Public and Power BI: These professional grade tools offer free versions that provide sophisticated visualization capabilities without requiring programming knowledge.

Getting Started with Professional Tools:

- Begin with pre-built templates and modify them for your specific data needs

- Focus on mastering 3-4 chart types thoroughly rather than using every available option

- Join online communities and forums where professionals share visualization techniques and troubleshooting advice

- Practice with public datasets before working with sensitive organizational data

- Create a portfolio of visualizations that demonstrate your ability to communicate insights clearly

Building a Visualization Portfolio
Creating a strong portfolio of visualizations involves selecting diverse examples that showcase your ability to turn data into clear, actionable insights. Each visualization should apply core design principles, clarity, honest representation, and strategic color use, while addressing real world problems relevant to your field. Pair visuals with brief narratives explaining the context, key findings, and implications to demonstrate data storytelling skills. Organize the portfolio professionally, using a clean format or interactive dashboards, and include details on tools used and outcomes achieved. Aim for quality over quantity by presenting 3 to 5 well-crafted examples that highlight versatility and practical impact.

Industry Applications of Data Visualization

<u>Human Resources and Organizational Development</u>:
HR professionals use data visualization to communicate workforce trends, training effectiveness, and employee satisfaction insights to leadership and staff.

Example:

> *Jennifer Middleton,* an HR coordinator at a mid-size tech company, noticed increasing employee turnover but struggled to identify patterns. Using Tableau Public, she created visualizations that showed turnover rates by department, tenure, and exit interview themes. The visuals revealed that turnover was highest among employees with 12-18 months of experience in customer-facing roles. This insight led to targeted retention initiatives that reduced turnover by 25% in affected departments.

<u>Education and Student Services</u>: Educational professionals use visualization to track student progress, resource utilization, and program effectiveness.

Example:

> *Marcus Pope,* a student success coordinator at a community college, wanted to improve first-year retention rates. He used Power BI to visualize "student engagement data library usage," tutoring center visits, club participation, and academic performance. The visualizations showed that students who engaged with support services within their first month had

significantly higher retention rates. This insight informed a proactive outreach program that increased first year retention by 15%.

<u>Nonprofit and Community Organizations:</u> Nonprofit professionals use data visualization to demonstrate impact, support fundraising efforts, and guide program development.

Example:

> *Lisa Knight*, a program manager at a food security nonprofit, needed to demonstrate the impact of their community garden program to potential funders. She created visualizations showing the relationship between garden participation, food access improvement, and community health metrics. The compelling visual story helped secure a $50,000 grant to expand the program to three additional neighborhoods.

Data Storytelling Techniques
Effective data visualization goes beyond creating attractive charts, it involves crafting narratives that guide viewers toward actionable insights.

Building Data Stories:

1. Establishing Context: Begin with background information that helps viewers understand why the data matters

2. Creating Tension: Highlight problems, opportunities, or questions that the data will address

3. Insight Revelation: Present key findings in a logical sequence that builds understanding

4. Action Orientation: Conclude with clear implications and recommended next steps

Visual Narrative Techniques:

- Annotate to guide viewer attention to important data points

- Create slide sequences that reveal information progressively

- Employ consistent visual themes that reinforce your message

- Include reference lines or benchmarks that provide context for data interpretation

- Design interactive elements that allow viewers to explore data at their own pace

Basic Coding for Everyone: Building Logic and Problem Solving Skills

Coding literacy has become as fundamental as mathematical. While not every professional needs to become a programmer, understanding basic coding concepts enhances problem solving abilities, improves communication with technical teams, and opens new possibilities for automation and efficiency.

Computational Thinking Skills
Before learning specific programming languages, developing computational thinking, the ability to break down complex problems into manageable components, provides the foundation for all technical work.

Core Computational Thinking Components:

> Decomposition: Breaking complex problems into smaller, manageable parts

> Pattern Recognition: Identifying similarities and recurring themes across different situations
> Abstraction: Focusing on essential features while ignoring irrelevant details

> Algorithm Design: Creating step by step procedures for solving problems

These skills apply far beyond programming. Project management, process improvement, strategic planning, and creative problem solving all benefit from computational thinking approaches.

Practical Programming Applications
Python for Everyday Automation: Python's readable syntax and extensive libraries make it ideal for professionals who want to automate routine tasks without becoming full time programmers.

Beginner Friendly Python Applications:

- Automating email sending and response categorization

- Processing and cleaning data from spreadsheets or surveys

- Creating simple web scrapers to gather information from websites

- Generating reports that pull data from multiple sources

- Building basic chatbots for customer service or internal communications

SQL for Data Management: Understanding SQL (Structured Query Language) enables professionals to work directly with databases, extracting insights and generating reports without depending on IT departments.

Essential SQL Skills for Non-Programmers:

- Writing SELECT statements to retrieve specific data

- Using WHERE clauses to filter information based on criteria

- Joining tables to combine information from multiple sources

- Creating aggregate functions (COUNT, SUM, AVERAGE) to summarize data

- Understanding how to export query results for use in other applications

JavaScript for Web Interaction: Basic JavaScript knowledge helps professionals understand how websites work and enables them to easily customize and automate web based tasks.

Practical JavaScript Applications:

- Customizing web based tools and platforms used in your industry

- Understanding how to work effectively with web developers on projects

- Creating simple interactive elements for presentations or websites

- Automating repetitive web based tasks using browser extensions

- Building basic web applications for team or personal use

Learning Pathways for Different Career Goals
<u>Business and Management Track:</u> Focus on tools that improve data analysis, process automation, and strategic decision-making.

Recommended Learning Sequence:

1. Excel/Google Sheets for advanced functions and macros

2. SQL for business intelligence and reporting

3. Python for data analysis using pandas and visualization libraries

4. Basic web development for understanding digital marketing and e-commerce

<u>Creative and Communications Track:</u> Emphasize tools that enhance creative work and improve audience engagement.

Recommended Learning Sequence:

1. HTML/CSS for web design and email marketing

2. JavaScript for interactive content and web animations

3. Python for social media automation and content analysis

4. Basic database management for content organization

<u>Healthcare and Research Track:</u> Concentrate on tools that support research, data analysis, and evidence based practice.

Recommended Learning Sequence:

1. R for statistical analysis and research

2. Python for data cleaning and visualization

3. SQL for managing research databases

4. Basic programming concepts for understanding health informatics systems

Overcoming Common Coding Learning Obstacles
"I'm Not a Math Person" Mindset: Many professionals avoid coding because they believe it requires advanced mathematical skills. In reality, most practical

programming uses basic logic and arithmetic that any college graduate can master.

Strategies for Math-Anxious Learners:

- Start with visual programming languages like Scratch that demonstrate logic without requiring syntax memorization

- Focus on practical projects that solve real problems in your field

- Join communities of non-technical professionals learning to code

- Emphasize the creative and problem solving aspects rather than mathematical computation

- Use online platforms with immediate feedback that make learning interactive and engaging

Time Management for Learning: Developing coding skills requires consistent practice, which can be challenging for busy professionals.

Effective Learning Strategies:

- Dedicate 20 to 30 minutes daily rather than attempting long weekend sessions

- Choose projects directly related to your current work responsibilities

- Find accountability partners or study groups within your professional network

- Use mobile apps and online platforms that allow learning during commutes or breaks

- Set specific, measurable goals (e.g., "automate my weekly report generation") rather than vague objectives

Final Flex

Digital fluency is no longer optional; it is a career imperative. Professionals who invest in cloud collaboration strategies, data storytelling techniques, and basic programming skills position themselves as agile contributors in any organization. Continuous learning and practical application of these tools ensure resilience in a rapidly changing digital landscape. By embracing these competencies, individuals not only meet current workplace demands but also future proof their careers against technological disruption.

Chapter 12: Cybersecurity for Remote Workers - Protecting Yourself and Your Organization

This chapter explores the critical importance of cybersecurity for remote workers in today's distributed work environment. It outlines the unique vulnerabilities introduced by home networks, personal devices, and blurred boundaries between professional and personal digital activities. Readers will learn about the most common threat categories such as phishing, unsecured networks, and device security gaps, and discover practical strategies for safeguarding sensitive information. The chapter also addresses industry specific considerations, incident response protocols, and the role remote professionals play in fostering a strong organizational security culture.

Remote work has expanded the cybersecurity threat landscape exponentially. Every home office becomes a potential entry point for cyber-attacks, making individual cybersecurity awareness crucial for organizational safety and career protection.

Understanding the Remote Work Threat Environment
Remote workers face unique cybersecurity challenges that don't exist in traditional office environments. Home networks often lack enterprise grade security protections, personal devices may have outdated security software, and the boundary between personal and professional digital activities becomes blurred.

Primary Threat Categories for Remote Workers:

<u>Phishing and Social Engineering</u>: Attackers exploit remote workers' isolation and increased digital communication dependence to trick them into revealing sensitive information.

<u>Unsecured Network Vulnerabilities</u>: Home Wi-Fi networks and public networks used by remote workers often lack adequate security controls.

<u>Device Security Gaps</u>: Personal devices used for work may lack proper security updates, antivirus protection, or access controls.

<u>Data Exposure Risks</u>: Working from various locations increases the risk of sensitive information being viewed by unauthorized individuals or stored insecurely.

Essential Cybersecurity Practices
Advanced Password Management - Beyond using strong passwords, remote workers need sophisticated password strategies that balance security with practicality.

Professional Password Strategies:

- Use enterprise grade password managers like 1Password Business or Bitwarden to generate and store unique passwords for all accounts

- Implement different password strategies for different risk levels (banking vs. social media)

- Enable multi-factor authentication on all work related accounts, using authenticator apps rather than SMS when possible

- Regularly audit and update passwords, especially after security breaches at companies where you have accounts

- Create secure password sharing procedures for team accounts and collaborative tools

Network Security for Remote Workers: Home and mobile network security requires proactive measures that many remote workers overlook.

Network Protection Strategies:

- Use VPN connections for all work related internet activity, not just when accessing company servers

- Configure home router security settings, including changing default passwords and enabling WPA3 encryption

- Create separate guest networks for visitors and devices to isolate work computers

- Understand how to identify and avoid unsecured public Wi-Fi networks

- Use mobile hotspots for sensitive work when secure Wi-Fi isn't available

Device Security and Management
Remote work devices need security configurations that protect both personal and professional information.

Device Protection Strategies:

- Enable automatic security updates for operating systems and essential applications

- Use full disk encryption to protect data if devices are lost or stolen

- Configure automatic screen locks with strong authentication methods

- Implement regular backup procedures for both personal and work data

- Install reputable antivirus software and keep it updated

- Use separate user accounts for work and personal activities when possible

Industry Specific Cybersecurity Considerations
<u>Financial Services Remote Work</u>

Financial industry remote workers handle highly sensitive data requiring enhanced security measures.

Example:

> *Max Burns,* a financial advisor working remotely, regularly updates his security training, and implements a multi-layered security approach. He uses dedicated work devices, encrypted external storage for client files, and

secure client communication portals. He also
establishes procedures for secure document
transmission and storage that exceed his firm's
minimum requirements. This proactive
approach protects Max's clients' sensitive
financial information and enables him to
provide excellent remote service.

<u>Healthcare Remote Work</u>

Healthcare professionals must maintain HIPAA
compliance while working remotely, requiring specific
security protocols.

Example:

Dr. Kenneth Remsen, conducting telemedicine
appointments from his home office, created a
secure remote work environment including
HIPAA compliant video conferencing software,
encrypted storage for patient records, secure
messaging systems for communicating with
colleagues, and physical privacy measures to
prevent unauthorized access to patient
information during virtual consultations.

<u>Education Remote Work</u>

Educational professionals need to protect student data
and institutional information while maintaining
accessibility for learning.

Example:

Professor Carol Beth Magic, teaching hybrid
courses, established security protocols including

secure video conferencing with waiting rooms and access controls, encrypted storage for student work and grades, secure communication channels for student consultations, and backup procedures for course materials and assignments. She also educated students about digital privacy and security relevant to their academic work.

Incident Response and Recovery
Recognizing Security Incidents:

Remote workers need skills to identify potential security breaches quickly and respond appropriately.

Incident Recognition Skills:

- Identify signs of compromised accounts (unexpected password reset emails, unfamiliar login notifications)

- Recognize malware symptoms (slow device performance, unexpected pop ups, unusual network activity)

- Spot phishing attempts in email, text messages, and phone calls

- Detect unauthorized access to files or accounts through audit logs and activity notifications

- Understand when and how to report suspected security incidents to employers and relevant authorities

Recovery Procedures:

When security incidents occur, quick and appropriate response minimizes damage and demonstrates professionalism.

Incident Response Steps:

1. Immediate Isolation: Disconnect affected devices from networks to prevent further damage

2. Assessment: Determine the scope and nature of the security incident

3. Documentation: Record details about the incident for investigation and reporting

4. Notification: Inform relevant parties (employers, clients, IT support) according to established protocols

5. Recovery: Implement steps to restore secure operations and prevent future incidents

6. Learning: Analyze the incident to improve future security practices and awareness

Building Organizational Cybersecurity Culture
Remote workers play crucial roles in building strong cybersecurity cultures within their organizations, even when working from distributed locations.

Security Advocacy Skills:

- Share cybersecurity best practices with colleagues through informal mentoring and formal training opportunities

- Participate actively in organizational security training and awareness programs

- Report security concerns and potential improvements to relevant stakeholders

- Model excellent security practices that inspire colleagues to elevate their own approaches

- Stay informed about emerging threats and security solutions relevant to your industry

Continuous Security Learning
Cybersecurity threats evolve constantly, requiring ongoing education and skill development.

Professional Development Strategies:

- Subscribe to cybersecurity newsletters and threat intelligence updates relevant to your industry

- Participate in cybersecurity webinars and professional development courses

- Join professional organizations that provide security training and networking opportunities

- Practice security skills through simulated phishing tests and security challenges

- Maintain awareness of regulatory requirements and compliance standards affecting your field

Integration and Advanced Applications
The true power of digital fluency emerges when cloud collaboration, data visualization, basic coding, and cybersecurity skills work together to solve complex professional challenges.

Cross Functional Digital Projects
Automated Reporting Systems: Combining coding skills with data visualization and cloud collaboration enables the creation of automated reporting systems that save time and improve accuracy.

Example:

> *Kevin Delasia*, a nonprofit program coordinator, used Python scripts to automatically collect data from multiple sources, including volunteer management systems, social media analytics, and donor databases. He then created Tableau visualizations to display impact metrics, shared his results with board members and funders through cloud-based dashboards, and implemented security protocols to protect donor and client information throughout the process.

Collaborative Research and Analysis

Digital fluency enables sophisticated research projects that span multiple team members and time zones.

Example:

> A cross functional marketing team used SQL to extract customer behavior data from multiple databases, created shared Jupyter notebooks for collaborative data analysis, built interactive visualizations that team members could explore independently, used version control systems to track analysis iterations, and maintained secure access controls throughout the research process.

Career Advancement Through Digital Innovation

Process Improvement Leadership: Professionals who can identify inefficiencies and propose digital solutions position themselves for leadership opportunities across all industries.

Strategic Technology Planning: Understanding how different digital tools integrate and support business objectives enables participation in strategic planning and technology adoption decisions.

Cross Departmental Bridge Building: Digital fluency enables effective communication between technical and nontechnical team members, creating valuable collaboration opportunities.

Final Flex

Remote work demands proactive cybersecurity measures to protect both individual careers and organizational integrity. Strong password management, secure network configurations, and device protection are non-negotiable essentials. Industry compliance requirements, such as HIPAA for healthcare or enhanced encryption for finance, must be prioritized. Professionals should remain vigilant for signs of breaches, respond swiftly to incidents, and commit to continuous learning through training and threat intelligence updates. By modeling best practices and advocating for security awareness, remote workers can transform cybersecurity from a personal responsibility into a shared organizational strength.

Chapter 13: Building Your Digital Brand

In today's hyper connected world, your digital brand is more than a profile, it's your professional reputation and the first impression most employers, collaborators, and clients will encounter. Building a compelling online presence requires more than posting content; it demands a strategic approach that integrates authenticity, consistency, and value across platforms. This chapter explores the fundamentals of digital branding, from optimizing LinkedIn and curating portfolios to creating thought leadership content and leveraging networking strategies. By applying these principles, you'll learn how to transform your digital footprint into a powerful career asset that attracts opportunities and establishes lasting credibility.

Your digital brand is your professional reputation in the online world. It's how potential employers, collaborators, and clients perceive your expertise, values, and professional potential. In today's interconnected professional landscape, a strong digital brand isn't optional; it's essential for career advancement and opportunity creation. This chapter provides comprehensive strategies for building an authentic, compelling digital presence that opens doors and accelerates career growth.

Understanding Digital Brand Fundamentals
Digital branding extends far beyond social media posting or website creation. It encompasses every digital touchpoint where your professional identity intersects with others' perceptions, from search engine results and social media profiles to online portfolio content and digital networking interactions.

The Modern Professional Identity Ecosystem
Your digital brand exists across multiple interconnected platforms and touchpoints, each serving different audiences and professional purposes. Understanding this ecosystem helps you create a cohesive, strategic presence rather than scattered, inconsistent profiles.

Core Digital Brand Components:

- Search Engine Presence: What appears when someone searches your name online
- Professional Platforms: LinkedIn, industry specific networking sites, professional directories
- Portfolio Spaces: Personal websites, GitHub repositories, Behance profiles, industry showcases
- Content Creation: Blog posts, articles, videos, podcasts, social media content
- Digital Networking: Online communities, professional forums, virtual events
- Reputation Management: Reviews, recommendations, testimonials, peer feedback

Brand Consistency Across Platforms: Effective digital brands maintain consistent messaging, visual identity, and professional positioning across all digital touchpoints while adapting content and tone for platform specific audiences and purposes.

Authentic Personal Branding vs. Self-Promotion
The most effective digital brands balance authentic self-expression with strategic professional positioning. This requires understanding the difference between genuine thought leadership and superficial self-promotion.

Authentic Digital Branding Principles:

- Value First Approach: Share insights, resources, and expertise that genuinely help others in your field
- Consistent Voice: Develop a professional communication style that reflects your personality and values
- Transparency: Be honest about your experience level, learning journey, and professional challenges
- Community Focus: Engage meaningfully with others rather than broadcasting one way promotional content
- Long term Perspective: Build relationships and reputation gradually rather than seeking immediate visibility

LinkedIn Optimization: Your Professional Home Base
LinkedIn serves as the foundation of most professionals' digital brands. Optimizing your LinkedIn presence requires understanding the platform's unique culture, algorithms, and networking opportunities.

Profile Optimization Strategy
Compelling Headline Creation: Your LinkedIn headline is prime real estate. It appears in search results, connection requests, and comments throughout the platform. Effective headlines go beyond job titles to communicate value and professional focus.

Headline Formula Examples:

- "Marketing Coordinator | Helping Nonprofits Increase Community Engagement Through Data Driven Storytelling"

- "Recent Business Graduate | Passionate About Sustainable Supply Chain Solutions and Operational Efficiency"

- "Software Engineer | Building Accessible Web Applications That Serve Diverse Communities"

Summary Section Excellence: The LinkedIn summary provides space for professional storytelling that humanizes your expertise while demonstrating value to potential connections.

Effective Summary Structure:

1. Opening Hook: Start with a compelling statement about your professional passion or unique perspective

2. Value Proposition: Clearly articulate what you bring to organizations and collaborators

3. Experience Highlights: Showcase key achievements and experiences that demonstrate your capabilities

4. Personal Touch: Include elements that make you memorable and relatable

5. Call to Action: Invite connections and conversations relevant to your professional goals

Experience Section Optimization: Transform basic job descriptions into achievement focused narratives that demonstrate impact and growth.

Experience Enhancement Techniques:

- Lead with action verbs that demonstrate initiative and leadership

- Quantify achievements whenever possible (percentages, dollar amounts, time savings)

- Include relevant keywords that align with your target opportunities

- Highlight collaborative projects and cross functional contributions

- Describe challenges overcome and lessons learned

Content Strategy for Professional Growth
Thought Leadership Content Creation: Thought leadership involves sharing insights, perspectives, and expertise that help others while establishing your professional reputation. Effective thought leadership content demonstrates knowledge while providing genuine value to your professional community.

Content Categories That Build Professional Reputation:

- Industry Insights: Share observations about trends, challenges, and opportunities in your field
- Lessons Learned: Discuss professional experiences and what they taught you
- Resource Sharing: Recommend books, articles, tools, or events that have helped your professional development
- Behind-the-Scenes: Offer glimpses into your work process, projects, or professional learning journey
- Community Recognition: Highlight colleagues' achievements and interesting work happening in your field

Engagement Strategy: Building a strong LinkedIn presence requires active participation in the platform's social aspects, not just content creation.

Engagement Best Practices:

- Comment thoughtfully on posts from colleagues and industry leaders

- Share others' content with your own insights and perspective added

- Respond promptly and meaningfully to comments on your own posts

- Participate in industry relevant LinkedIn groups and discussions

- Send personalized connection requests that reference shared interests or experiences

Advanced LinkedIn Features

LinkedIn Articles vs. Posts: Understanding what format pairs best with you content will maximize your reach and impact.

LinkedIn Articles:

- Use for longer form content (800+ words) that provides comprehensive insights

- Ideal for thought leadership pieces, detailed case studies, or educational content

- Better for SEO and evergreen content that remains relevant over time

- More likely to be discovered by people outside your immediate network

LinkedIn Posts:

- Use for timely updates, brief insights, and conversational content

- Better for engagement and real time interaction with your network

- Ideal for sharing quick wins, asking questions, or starting discussions

- More visible in immediate connections' feeds

LinkedIn Events and Newsletters: Advanced LinkedIn features enable community building and thought leadership development.

Professional Event Creation:

- Host virtual networking events for professionals in your field

- Organize industry discussion panels or expert interviews

- Create professional development workshops or skill sharing sessions

- Facilitate alumni networking or mentorship connection events

Newsletter Publishing:

- Develop regular content series that followers can subscribe to

- Share consistent insights on industry trends or professional development

- Build a dedicated audience interested in your expertise and perspective

Content Strategy Development
Niche Expertise Identification: Successful thought leadership requires focusing on specific areas where you can provide unique value and insights.

Expertise Development Process:

1. Experience Inventory: Catalog your educational background, work experiences, projects, and unique perspectives

2. Intersection Analysis: Identify areas where your experiences intersect in unique ways

3. Audience Research: Understand what challenges and questions your target professional community faces

4. Value Gap Analysis: Identify topics where you can provide insights that aren't readily available elsewhere

5. Passion Alignment: Focus on areas where your genuine interest will sustain long term content creation

Content Calendar Planning: Consistent thought leadership requires strategic planning and systematic content creation.

Content Planning Framework:

- Foundational Content: Establish your perspective on key industry topics through comprehensive pieces

- Trending Topics: Provide timely commentary on current events and industry developments

- Educational Content: Share knowledge and skills that help others in their professional development

- Personal Insights: Offer lessons learned from your own professional experiences and challenges

- Community Content: Highlight others' work and foster discussion within your professional network

Platform Specific Content Strategies

LinkedIn Article Writing: LinkedIn articles provide opportunities for substantial thought leadership content that reaches professional audiences.

Effective LinkedIn Article Strategies:

- Hook Heavy Headlines: Create titles that immediately communicate value and relevance to your target audience

- Problem Solution Structure: Address specific challenges your audience faces and provide actionable solutions

- Story Integration: Use personal anecdotes and case studies to illustrate professional insights

- Action Oriented Conclusions: End articles with specific steps readers can take to apply your insights

- Discussion Facilitation: Ask questions and encourage comments to foster community engagement

Industry Blog Contributions: Writing for established industry publications expands your reach and credibility within professional communities.

Guest Writing Strategies:

- Publication Research: Identify blogs and publications that serve your target audience

- Editorial Calendar Analysis: Understand what types of content each publication prioritizes

- Pitch Development: Create compelling article proposals that align with publication goals and audience needs

- Relationship Building: Develop ongoing relationships with editors and other contributors

- Cross Promotion: Leverage guest posts to drive traffic to your own platforms and build your network

Video and Podcast Content: Audio and video content creation provides opportunities to reach audiences who prefer multimedia learning and engagement.

Multimedia Content Strategies:

- Educational Series: Create ongoing video or podcast series that provide consistent value to your audience

- Interview Formats: Host conversations with other professionals to share diverse perspectives and build networks

- Process Documentation: Show your work process or problem solving approach through video tutorials or case studies

- Conference Speaking: Seek opportunities to present at industry events and share that content across digital platforms

- Collaborative Content: Partner with other professionals to create content that provides multiple perspectives

Content Quality and Authenticity
Research and Fact Checking: Thought leadership content must be accurate, well researched, and intellectually honest to build lasting credibility.

Content Accuracy Standards:

- Source Citation: Properly attribute ideas, data, and insights to original sources

- Fact Verification: Double check statistics, claims, and factual assertions before publishing

- Update Management: Revise content when new information changes your conclusions or recommendations

- Expertise Boundaries: Clearly communicate the limits of your knowledge and experience

- Peer Review: Seek feedback from knowledgeable colleagues before publishing significant content

Voice and Personality Development: Authentic thought leadership balances professional expertise with genuine personality and individual perspective.

Voice Development Techniques:

- Conversational Tone: Write as if you're explaining concepts to a colleague rather than delivering a formal presentation

- Personal Experience Integration: Share relevant stories and experiences that illustrate your points

- Honest Vulnerability: Acknowledge mistakes, learning experiences, and areas where you're still developing expertise

- Consistent Values: Let your professional values and priorities come through in your content choices and perspectives

- Unique Perspective: Emphasize what makes your viewpoint different from others in your field

Portfolio Development: Showcasing Your Professional Value

Digital portfolios have evolved beyond creative fields to become essential tools for professionals across all industries. An effective portfolio demonstrates not just what you've done, but how you think, solve problems, and create value.

Multi Format Portfolio Strategy

Platform Selection: Different industries and career goals require different portfolio approaches and platforms.

Portfolio Platform Options:

- Personal Websites: Maximum customization and control, ideal for establishing thought leadership

- Industry Specific Platforms: Behance for designers, GitHub for developers, Dribbble for creative professionals

- Integrated Platforms: Notion, WordPress, Squarespace for flexible, professional presentations

- Social Platforms: Instagram for visual portfolios, YouTube for video content, Medium for written thought leadership

Content Curation Strategy: Effective portfolios tell coherent professional stories rather than simply displaying all available work.

Curation Principles:

- Quality Over Quantity: Showcase 3 - 5 exceptional projects rather than overwhelming visitors with everything you've ever created

- Narrative Arc: Arrange projects to show professional growth, skill development, or thematic expertise

- Audience Relevance: Tailor portfolio content to the specific opportunities and audiences you're targeting

- Process Documentation: Include insights into your thinking process, problem solving approach, and collaborative methods

- Results Emphasis: Highlight outcomes, impacts, and lessons learned from featured projects

Industry Specific Portfolio Approaches
Business and Consulting Portfolios: Business professionals need portfolios that demonstrate analytical thinking, strategic problem solving, and measurable impact.

Business Portfolio Elements:

- Case Studies: Detailed analyses of projects or challenges you've addressed, including methodology and outcomes

- Data Analysis Projects: Examples of how you've used data to inform decisions or solve problems

- Process Improvements: Documentation of systems or workflows you've optimized

- Strategic Planning: Examples of planning documents, market analyses, or strategic recommendations you've developed

- Leadership Experiences: Descriptions of teams you've led or initiatives you've spearheaded

Example:

> *Sarah Chen*, a supply chain management student, created a portfolio case study documenting her internship project, for which she helped a local manufacturer optimize their inventory management. Her portfolio included problem identification, data analysis methodology, stakeholder interview insights, proposed solutions, implementation planning, and projected cost savings. This comprehensive presentation helped her secure full time offers from three consulting firms.

Technology and Engineering Portfolios: Technical professionals need portfolios that demonstrate coding ability, system design thinking, and problem solving skills.

Technical Portfolio Elements:

- Code Repositories: Well documented GitHub projects that show coding skills and project management abilities

- System Design Documentation: Explanations of technical architecture decisions and trade offs

- Problem Solving Examples: Descriptions of technical challenges and your solution approaches

- Collaboration Projects: Examples of team based development work and your contributions

- Continuous Learning: Documentation of new technologies you've explored and skills you've developed

Example:

> *Marcus Pope*, a computer science student, built a portfolio website showcasing a web application he developed to help local nonprofits manage volunteer scheduling. His portfolio included the full codebase on GitHub, documentation of the development process, user testing results, and reflections on technical decisions. The project demonstrated both technical skills and social impact awareness, leading to internship offers at both tech companies and nonprofit organizations.

Creative and Communications Portfolios: Creative professionals need portfolios that demonstrate artistic vision, technical execution, and strategic thinking about audience and impact.

Creative Portfolio Elements:

- Project Context: Background information about client needs, target audiences, and creative objectives

- Creative Process: Documentation of ideation, iteration, and refinement processes

- Technical Execution: Examples of skill in relevant software, techniques, and production methods

- Impact Measurement: Data on audience engagement, client satisfaction, or campaign effectiveness

- Cross Media Experience: Examples of work across different formats, platforms, and audiences

Example:

Elena Shepherd, a communications major, created a comprehensive campaign portfolio for a university sustainability initiative she led. Her portfolio included audience research, message development, multi-platform content creation, event planning documentation, and campaign effectiveness metrics. The strategic approach impressed potential employers and led to a full time offer in corporate communications.

Portfolio Presentation Excellence

Visual Design Principles: Even non-designers benefit from understanding basic visual design principles that make portfolios more professional and engaging.

Design Best Practices:

- Consistent Visual Identity: Use consistent colors, fonts, and styling throughout your portfolio

- White Space Usage: Avoid cluttered layouts that overwhelm visitors or obscure your content

- Hierarchy Creation: Use size, color, and positioning to guide visitors through your content logically

- Mobile Optimization: Ensure your portfolio displays well on phones and tablets

- Loading Speed: Optimize images and content for fast loading times

Storytelling Through Portfolio Structure: Effective portfolios guide visitors through intentional narratives about your professional development and capabilities.

Narrative Structure Options:

- Chronological Growth: Show professional development over time through increasingly sophisticated projects

- Skill Based Organization: Group projects by key competencies or areas of expertise

- Challenge Solution Format: Organize around problems you've solved or challenges you've addressed

- Industry Application: Structure around different sectors or applications of your skills

- Process Focused: Emphasize your problem solving methodology and thinking process using SOLVE

Online Networking Strategies

Digital networking has evolved far beyond collecting LinkedIn connections. Effective online networking involves building genuine professional relationships, contributing meaningfully to professional communities, and creating mutual value through digital interactions.

Strategic Network Building

Quality vs. Quantity Approach: Successful digital networking prioritizes meaningful connections over large contact lists.

Relationship Building Priorities:

- Mutual Interest Connections: Focus on people who share professional interests, challenges, or goals

- Industry Diverse Networks: Build connections across different levels, functions, and perspectives within your field

- Geographic Expansion: Use digital platforms to connect with professionals beyond your immediate geographic area

- Mentor and Peer Balance: Cultivate relationships with both experienced professionals and peers at similar career stages

- Value Exchange Mindset: When networking, highlight what you can contribute, not just what you hope to gain

Professional Community Participation: Active participation in online professional communities builds reputation and relationships organically.

Community Engagement Strategies:

- Consistent Contribution: Regularly share insights, resources, and helpful responses in professional forums and groups

- Question Asking: Pose thoughtful questions that generate meaningful discussions and demonstrate your engagement with industry issues

- Resource Sharing: Recommend articles, tools, events, and opportunities that benefit community members

- Celebration and Recognition: Acknowledge others' achievements and interesting work publicly

- Event Participation: Attend virtual conferences, webinars, and networking events actively rather than passively

Platform Specific Networking Approaches
LinkedIn Networking Excellence: LinkedIn networking requires understanding the platform's professional culture and leveraging its specific features effectively.

Advanced LinkedIn Networking:

- Strategic Connection Requests: Send personalized invitations that reference shared interests, mutual connections, or specific reasons for connecting

- Follow Up Messaging: Develop systems for maintaining contact with new connections through valuable content sharing and periodic check-ins

- Group Participation: Join and actively participate in LinkedIn groups relevant to your industry and interests

- Event Networking: Use LinkedIn Events to connect with attendees before, during, and after professional gatherings

- Alumni Network Activation: Leverage university and previous employer networks for warm introductions and career advice

X Professional Engagement: X (formerly Twitter) enables real time professional conversations and thought leadership sharing within industry communities.

X Networking Strategies:

- Industry Chat Participation: Join weekly X chats relevant to your field using hashtags and scheduled times

- Thoughtful Commenting: Add meaningful responses to tweets from industry leaders and peers

- Content Curation: Share and comment on articles, research, and insights that benefit your professional network

- Live Event Engagement: Participate in X conversations during conferences and industry events

- Thread Creation: Use X threads to share longer form insights and start deeper conversations

Industry Specific Platforms: Different fields have specialized networking platforms that offer unique opportunities for professional connection.

Platform Examples by Industry:

- Healthcare: Doximity for physicians, Figure 1 for medical case discussions

- Academia: ResearchGate for research collaboration, Academia.edu for paper sharing

- Design: Dribbble for creative portfolio sharing, Behance for project showcasing

- Technology: GitHub for code collaboration, Stack Overflow for technical problem solving

- Legal: Martindale - Hubbell for attorney networking, Legal Compass for law firm insights

Networking Follow Through and Relationship Maintenance

Systematic Relationship Management: Effective networkers develop systems for maintaining connections and nurturing professional relationships over time.

Relationship Management Systems:

- Contact Database Creation: Maintain organized records of professional contacts including conversation history and mutual interests

- Regular Check In Scheduling: Establish routines for periodic outreach to maintain relationship warmth

- Value Add Communications: Share opportunities, introductions, and resources that benefit your network connections

- Professional Update Sharing: Keep your network informed about your career progress and professional developments

- Introduction Facilitation: Connect people in your network who would benefit from knowing each other

Professional Reciprocity: Sustainable networking requires balance between receiving help and providing value to others in your professional network.

Reciprocity Strategies:

- Skill Sharing: Offer your expertise to help others with projects or challenges

- Opportunity Forwarding: Share job openings, freelance opportunities, and professional development resources

- Introduction Making: Connect people who would benefit from knowing each other

- Content Amplification: Share and promote your connections' professional content and achievements

  Mentoring Contribution: Provide guidance and support to professionals earlier in their careers

Measuring Digital Brand Success
Effective digital brand building requires systematic measurement and continuous improvement based on data and feedback.

Reach and Engagement Analytics: Most digital platforms provide analytics that help you understand how your content and profile perform.

Key Metrics to Track:

- Profile Views and Search Appearances: How often people discover your profile through search or recommendations

- Content Engagement: Likes, comments, shares, and clicks on your posts and articles

- Network Growth: Quality and quantity of new professional connections over time

- Website Traffic: Visitors to your portfolio or personal website, including traffic sources and page views

- Content Performance: Which topics and formats generate the most engagement and reach

Professional Opportunity Indicators: The ultimate measure of digital brand success is its impact on career opportunities and professional growth.

- Inbound Inquiries: Job opportunities, collaboration requests, and speaking invitations that come to you

- Network Referrals: Opportunities that come through your professional network connections

- Thought Leadership Recognition: Invitations to contribute content, speak at events, or participate in industry discussions

- Professional Advancement: Promotions, career changes, and salary improvements influenced by your digital presence

- Industry Recognition: Awards, nominations, or public recognition for your professional contributions

Qualitative Feedback

Professional Reputation Assessment: Understanding how others perceive your digital brand provides valuable insights for improvement and refinement.

Reputation Evaluation Methods:

- Direct Feedback Requests: Ask trusted colleagues and mentors for honest assessments of your online presence

- Search Result Analysis: Regularly search your name to understand what information appears and how it represents you

- Social Listening: Monitor mentions of your name and work across social platforms

- Professional Reference Conversations: Include digital brand topics in reference and networking conversations

- Industry Peer Feedback: Seek input from others in your field about your thought leadership and professional positioning

Brand Alignment Assessment: Regularly evaluate whether your digital brand accurately represents your professional goals and authentic self.

Alignment Evaluation Questions:

- Does your digital presence accurately reflect your professional values and priorities?

- Are you attracting the types of opportunities and connections you want?

- Do you feel comfortable and authentic in your online professional interactions?

- Is your digital brand helping you achieve your short term and long term career goals?

- Are you providing genuine value to your professional community through your digital presence?

Advanced Digital Brand Strategies
As your career progresses, your digital brand can become increasingly sophisticated and strategically powerful.

Personal Brand Evolution
Career Stage Adaptation: Your digital brand strategy should evolve as you progress from early career to senior leadership roles.

Early Career Focus:

- Learning Documentation: Share your professional development journey and learning experiences

- Skill Demonstration: Showcase projects and achievements that prove your capabilities

- Network Building: Focus on connecting with peers, mentors, and industry professionals

- Industry Integration: Demonstrate your understanding of and engagement with industry trends and challenges

Mid-Career Development:

- Expertise Positioning: Establish yourself as knowledgeable in specific areas of your field

- Thought Leadership: Share insights and perspectives based on your growing experience

- Mentoring Presence: Begin supporting earlier career professionals in your network

- Strategic Networking: Build relationships that support both your current role and future aspirations

Senior Leadership Brand:

- Industry Influence: Position yourself as a leader who shapes industry conversations and trends

- Cross Industry Perspective: Share insights that bridge different sectors and professional communities

- Legacy Building: Focus on contributions that will have lasting impact on your field

- Next Generation Development: Actively mentor and develop emerging professionals

Global Digital Brand Considerations

Cultural Sensitivity: As digital platforms connect professionals globally, understanding cultural differences in professional communication becomes increasingly important.

Global Brand Strategies:

- Cultural Adaptation: Adjust communication styles and content approaches for different cultural contexts

- Time Zone Awareness: Consider when you post content and engage with global audiences

- Language Accessibility: Use clear, straightforward language that translates well across cultures

- Local Relevance: Include global perspectives while maintaining relevance to your primary professional community

- Inclusive Representation: Ensure your digital brand reflects awareness of and respect for diverse professional perspectives

Future Proofing Your Digital Brand
Digital platforms and professional networking trends evolve rapidly. Building digital brand strategies that can adapt to platform changes will elicit long-term career benefits.

Platform Independence
Content Ownership: Maintain control over your professional content and brand assets rather than relying entirely on third party platforms.

Content Control Strategies:

- Personal Website Maintenance: Keep an updated personal website that serves as your brand headquarters

- Content Backup: Regularly download and backup content you create on various platforms

- Email List Building: Develop direct communication channels with your professional network

- Multi-Platform Presence: Avoid becoming overdependent on any single platform for your digital brand

- Brand Asset Creation: Develop logos, color schemes, and visual elements you can use across platforms

Emerging Technology Integration
Staying Current with Digital Trends: Maintaining digital brand relevance requires users to be aware of and open to adapting to new technologies and platforms.

Technology Adaptation Strategies:

- Selective Early Adoption: Experiment with new platforms while maintaining focus on existing tools that have proven merit

- Professional Development Investment: Continuously develop digital skills that support your brand and career goals

- Industry Trend Monitoring: Stay informed about evolving digital tools and platforms in your specific field

- Network Learning: Learn from how other professionals in your network adapt to and leverage new technologies

- Strategic Patience: Avoid jumping on every new trend while remaining open to genuine opportunities for brand enhancement

Building a strong digital brand is not a one-time project but an ongoing professional practice that requires authenticity, consistency, and strategic thinking. The professionals who invest in thoughtful digital brand development create lasting advantages that compound over time, opening opportunities and building relationships that fuel entire careers.

Final Flex
Your digital brand should embody a natural extension of your professional self. Not a manufactured persona, but a strategic presentation of your authentic expertise, values, and professional potential. Start with small, consistent steps: optimize your LinkedIn profile, share one thoughtful piece of content each week, engage meaningfully with your network, and gradually expand your digital presence as you grow more comfortable and sophisticated in your approach.

Investing in digital brand building pays dividends throughout your career, creating a professional reputation that works for you even when you're not actively job searching or networking. In an increasingly digital professional world, your online presence often forms first impressions and opens doors long before you meet people face to face.

Remember that building a strong digital brand is ultimately about adding value to your professional community while advancing your own career goals. The most successful digital brands are those that help others while authentically representing the unique professional value you bring to your field.

Chapter 14: Career & Self Development: Creating Opportunities

Career success is not a matter of chance. It's the result of intentional growth, strategic networking, and continuous self-improvement. This chapter explores how professionals can create opportunities by building strong networks, leveraging mentorship, and embracing lifelong learning. Readers will discover practical strategies for attending industry events, engaging on digital platforms, and forming meaningful workplace relationships. The chapter also highlights the importance of mentorship, both formal and informal, and offers guidance on setting clear career goals, pursuing certifications, and stepping into leadership roles. By applying these principles, individuals can accelerate their development, stand out in competitive markets, and position themselves for long term success.

Career success doesn't happen overnight. It requires continuous learning, networking, and personal development. Employers appreciate candidates who proactively seek growth opportunities.

Why Employers Appreciate Candidates Who Proactively Seek Growth Opportunities
In today's fast-paced and competitive job market, employers value candidates who actively pursue professional growth. Companies don't just look for individuals who meet the job description, they want employees who take initiative, continuously improve

their skills, and contribute meaningfully to the organization. Those who build strong networks, seek mentorship, and invest in career progression demonstrate ambition, adaptability, and long term potential.

How to Build a Strong Professional Network
A solid professional network is essential for career success. Networking connects individuals with industry leaders, opens doors to job opportunities, and facilitates knowledge sharing. Employers appreciate candidates who use their connections strategically to advance their careers and bring value to their organizations.

1. Attending Industry Events and Conferences

Engaging in professional gatherings such as seminars, networking events, and trade conferences provides opportunities to meet industry experts and potential employers.

Example:

> *Jamal Laurier*, a recent marketing graduate from MacTech University, attended the American Advertising Federation's national conference in Chicago. Passionate about brand strategy and digital media, Jamal used the summit to learn from industry leaders and connect with professionals beyond the classroom.

During a breakout session on AI in advertising, Jamal struck up a conversation with *Rose Sinclair*, a senior account executive at Ogilvy. They discussed emerging trends, shared insights from recent campaigns, and exchanged contact information. Impressed by Jamal's curiosity and professionalism, Rose later invited him to apply for Ogilvy's competitive summer internship program.

A few weeks after the summit, Jamal interviewed and was offered the internship; the opportunity became a launching pad for his career in agency marketing.

Attending professional events can lead to meaningful connections and open doors. For young professionals, especially those early in their careers, showing up, engaging thoughtfully, and following up can turn a single conversation into a life changing opportunity.

Best Practices:

- Participate in panel discussions and workshops.
- Exchange contact information and follow up with connections.
- Engage in meaningful conversations rather than just handing out business cards.

2. Leveraging Online Networking Platforms

Digital networking platforms such as LinkedIn, X (Twitter), Instagram, Tik Tok, and industry specific forums are powerful tools for building connections.

Example:

> *Elena Shepherd*, a software developer based in Jersey City and a MacTech University alumna, had a growing interest in artificial intelligence and its ethical tech design applications. While working full-time at a mid-sized fintech company, she began regularly posting on LinkedIn, sharing insights from AI conferences, commenting on emerging tools like generative models, and writing short reflections on responsible AI development.
>
> One of her posts, a thoughtful take on the implications of AI in hiring algorithms, sparked a lively discussion. Among those who engaged was *Marcus Pope*, a senior recruiter at a leading AI startup, and *Dr. Priya Desai*, a well-known voice in AI ethics. Impressed by Elena's clarity and perspective, Marcus reached out to discuss a potential role, while Dr. Nair invited her to contribute to a panel on inclusive AI design.
>
> What started as casual engagement turned into real professional momentum. By consistently contributing to conversations on AI, Elena built credibility, expanded her network, and opened doors to new career opportunities.

Best Practices:

- Maintain an updated LinkedIn profile highlighting expertise and achievements.
- Join relevant groups to stay informed about industry trends.
- Connect with professionals and personalize messages when reaching out.

3. Establishing Meaningful Workplace Relationships

Networking doesn't just happen externally, it's also vital within a company. Building strong relationships with colleagues, supervisors, and cross functional teams enhances career prospects.

Example:

> At MacTech University, *Alice Han*, an entry level data analyst in the Office of Institutional Research, was assigned to support a strategic enrollment project led by *Dr. Nadine Sobel*, Vice President for Academic Affairs. While her initial role focused on compiling reports, Alice regularly went beyond expectations; asking thoughtful questions, proposing data visualizations, and volunteering to take on additional tasks.

> Her proactive approach caught Dr. Sobel's attention. Impressed by her initiative, he began inviting Alice to higher-level planning meetings and introduced her to *Nina Bajaj*, a senior business analyst, who became an informal

mentor. Through these relationships, Alice gained exposure to university wide strategy, sharpened her analytical skills, and built confidence in presenting her work.

Within a year, Alice was promoted to a mid-level analyst role and asked to co-lead a dashboard development project for the Student Success division.

Employers value employees who actively engage with leadership, leverage their relationships, seek mentorship, and contribute meaningfully to their teams. By building relationships and showing initiative, young professionals accelerate their learning and open doors to career advancement.

Finding Mentors and Leveraging Mentorship Opportunities
Seeking guidance from experienced professionals accelerates career development. A mentor provides insight, career advice, and encouragement, helping employees avoid common pitfalls and refine their skills.

1. Identifying the Right Mentor

A good mentor should be knowledgeable, approachable, and invested in guiding others. Finding a mentor within the organization or industry provides career guidance tailored to specific goals.

Example:

At a networking event hosted by MacTech University's Thunderdome School of Business, *Audrey Palmer*, a junior financial analyst and recent graduate, attended a panel on ethical investing and leadership in finance. Eager to grow beyond her entry-level role, Audrey stayed after the session to speak with *Luis Hernandez*, a senior executive at a global investment firm and one of the panelists.

Impressed by Audrey's thoughtful questions and curiosity, Luis offered to stay in touch. Over the following months, they met periodically for coffee chats and virtual check-ins. Luis shared insights on leadership development, investment frameworks, and how to navigate high stakes decision making in a fast paced industry.

With his guidance, Audrey refined her analytical approach, gained confidence in presenting to senior stakeholders, and eventually earned a promotion to associate analyst. More importantly, she developed a clearer vision for her career path and a trusted mentor to help guide it.

This example shows how identifying the right mentor, someone whose experience aligns with your aspirations, can accelerate growth, build confidence, and open doors. Employers value professionals who take initiative to learn from others and invest in their own development.

Best Practices:

- Choose mentors aligned with career aspirations.
- Communicate expectations and establish a structured mentorship process.
- Be receptive to feedback and apply lessons learned.

2. Engaging in Formal Mentorship Programs

Many companies and professional organizations offer structured mentorship programs where experienced professionals guide early career employees.

Example:

Mac & Fromage Engineering, a mid-sized civil and environmental engineering firm based in Boston, runs a structured mentorship program designed to accelerate the development of new hires.

Program Structure: During their first 12 months, new engineers are paired with senior mentors. Mentors are selected based on project alignment and technical expertise.

Mentor Example: *Jessica Lin*, a Principal Structural Engineer with 18 years of experience, mentors *Carlos Ramirez*, a recent graduate from Northeastern University. Carlos is working on bridge rehabilitation projects, and Jessica guides him through design reviews, client meetings, and field inspections.

Learning Outcomes:

- Carlos gains hands on experience with AutoCAD and structural modeling software.

- He learns how to navigate regulatory codes and communicate with municipal clients.

- Jessica provides weekly feedback and helps Carlos set quarterly goals for skill development.

Impact:

- Carlos reports increased confidence and faster onboarding.

- The firm sees improved retention and performance among mentees.

- Mentors like Jessica also benefit by developing leadership and coaching skills.

Employers appreciate candidates who actively seek mentorship, as it demonstrates a commitment to self-improvement and leadership potential. Even if there are no structured programs offered, seek mentorship.

3. Learning from Multiple Mentors

Employees should not limit themselves to just one mentor. Learning from multiple perspectives broadens knowledge and offers diverse guidance.

Example:

Ava Thompson, a junior at MacTech University majoring in Business Administration, dreams of launching a sustainable fashion startup. Through RamConnect, she builds a personalized mentorship team that supports her across key areas of entrepreneurship:

- Leadership Mentor: *Dr. Renee Caldwell*, a MacTech alumna and current VP of Organizational Development at Patagonia, meets with Ava monthly to discuss team building, ethical leadership, and navigating startup culture. Renee shares strategies for building inclusive company values and managing early stage teams.

- Financial Planning Mentor: *Marcus Lee*, a CPA and founder of GreenLedger Consulting, helps Ava understand budgeting, forecasting, and investor relations. He guides her through creating a financial model for her business plan and introduces her to tools like QuickBooks and PitchBook.

- Business Operations Mentor: *Jorge Alvarez*, COO of a New York based e-commerce logistics firm, offers insights into supply chain management, vendor negotiations, and scaling operations. Jorge connects Ava with local manufacturers and helps her evaluate fulfillment strategies.

Seeking mentorship expands professional knowledge and demonstrates initiative, making employees valuable contributors to their workplace.

Strategies for Career Progression and Self Improvement

Employers value individuals who prioritize continuous learning, professional growth, and skill development. Staying updated in an evolving job market demonstrates adaptability and ambition, two traits highly sought after by companies.

1. Setting Clear Career Goals

Defining career objectives helps employees create a roadmap for success. Short term and long term goals guide professional development and provide measurable milestones.

Example:

> *Lena Brooks*, a content writer at BrightWave Media, joined the company in 2021 after graduating from Syracuse University with a degree in Communications. From the start, Lena set a clear goal: to become a Senior Editor within five years.
>
> To actively shape her career path, Lena created a personal development plan with three key pillars:

1. Skill Refinement
   Lena dedicated time each week to improving her writing, studying SEO strategies, mastering AP style, and experimenting with storytelling formats. She also sought regular feedback from her editor, *James Kittlesworth*, to identify areas for growth.

2. Professional Development
   She attended writing workshops hosted by organizations like Content Marketing Institute and NYC Writers Collective, where she learned advanced editing techniques and networked with industry professionals. She also completed a certificate in digital publishing through Coursera.

3. Portfolio Building
   Lena took initiative to lead high impact projects, including a series on climate tech startups that earned BrightWave a Webby nomination. She curated a portfolio showcasing her versatility, from blog posts and white papers to video scripts and social media campaigns.

Employers appreciate goal-oriented professionals who actively shape their career paths instead of waiting for opportunities to appear.

2. Pursuing Continuing Education and Certifications

Practicing lifelong learning, such as taking courses, earning certifications, or attending workshops, boosts expertise and marketability.

Example:

> *Derrick Chen*, an IT specialist at MetroCore Solutions, had been working in desktop support and systems administration for several years. While he was technically proficient, Derrick wanted to future proof his career and move into more strategic, high impact roles in cloud infrastructure.
>
> In 2024, Derrick set a goal to become a Cloud Solutions Architect within two years. To get there, he enrolled in a structured learning path and earned multiple certifications, including:
>
> - AWS Certified Solutions Architect, Associate
> - Microsoft Azure Administrator
> - Google Cloud Digital Leader
>
> He supplemented his learning with hands on labs through platforms like A Cloud Guru and Coursera, and began applying his new skills to internal projects, migrating legacy systems to AWS and optimizing cloud storage costs.

Best Practices:

- Enroll in professional development courses.

- Stay updated on industry trends through research and training.
- Obtain relevant certifications to increase expertise and credibility.

3. Seeking Out Challenges and Leadership Opportunities

Employees who volunteer for high impact projects, propose innovative solutions, and step into leadership roles showcase initiative and leadership potential.

Example:

> *Jordan Carlson*, a junior manager at Crestline Analytics, noticed that his team spent excessive time compiling weekly performance reports. Rather than waiting for upper management to address the inefficiency, Jordan took initiative.
>
> He proposed a new workflow using automated dashboards built in Power BI, which would pull real time data from the company's CRM and reduce reporting time by 60%. He also suggested a shared task tracker to improve transparency and accountability across departments.
>
> Jordan implemented the changes with his company's IT team and trained his colleagues on the new system. Within two months, the team's productivity noticeably improved, and cross-functional communication became smoother.

Jordan's proactive approach earned him recognition from the Director of Operations, *Hollie Schitt*, who praised his initiative during a quarterly leadership meeting. Shortly after, Jordan was promoted to Operations Manager, with expanded responsibilities and a seat at strategic planning sessions.

Employers value individuals who take on challenges, think critically, and contribute beyond assigned tasks, as it benefits both the employee and the company.

Final Flex

Employers prioritize candidates who seek career growth, embrace learning opportunities, and build strong professional relationships. Candidates who network effectively, find mentorship, and actively develop their skills not only advance their own careers but also contribute to workplace innovation, leadership, and long term success.

By proactively shaping their professional journeys, individuals increase their value, strengthen their career potential, and stand out in competitive job markets. The key to success is never settling! Continuous growth is the true mark of a high achieving professional.

Chapter 15: Leadership: Inspiring Growth and Innovation

Leadership is a dynamic skill that transcends job titles and formal authority. In today's workplace, employers value professionals who take initiative, communicate effectively, and inspire collaboration. This chapter explores how individuals at any career stage can develop leadership capabilities by owning projects, fostering positive team cultures, and applying strategic thinking to solve complex challenges. Through real world examples and best practices, readers will learn how leading by example, motivating colleagues, and making informed decisions not only drive innovation and productivity but also position them as indispensable contributors to organizational success.

Leadership isn't just for managers. Every employee has the opportunity to lead in some way.

Why Employers Value Candidates Who Take Initiative, Motivate Others, and Bring Solutions
Employers seek professionals who do more than just complete tasks. They want individuals who take initiative, inspire colleagues, and bring solutions to challenges.

Young professionals can stand out by developing leadership skills at any career stage, leading by example, and mastering strategic decision making. Regardless of experience level, taking ownership, guiding teams, and making well-informed decisions increase productivity, drive success, and foster workplace innovation.

Developing Leadership Skills at Any Career Stage
1. Taking Ownership of Tasks and Projects

Employees who take initiative by volunteering for challenging projects, proposing improvements, or independently solving issues demonstrate leadership potential.

Example:

> Samantha Reyes, a junior data analyst at HorizonTech Solutions, had been with the company for just under a year when she noticed a recurring issue: the team's weekly performance reports were being compiled manually using spreadsheets from multiple departments. The process was time consuming, error prone, and often delayed decision making.
>
> Instead of waiting for someone to address the inefficiency, Samantha took initiative. In the evenings, she researched reporting automation tools and best practices. After evaluating several options, she proposed a solution using Google Data Studio integrated with the company's CRM and project management software.
>
> She created a prototype dashboard that:
>
> - Automatically pulled real time data from multiple sources

- Visualized key performance indicators (KPIs)
- Allowed managers to filter by team, project, and time period

Samantha presented the solution to her manager, *Daniel Cho*, who was impressed by both the functionality and her initiative. After a brief pilot, the dashboard was adopted company wide.

Best Practices:

- Speak up when identifying opportunities for improvement.
- Show confidence in handling responsibilities without excessive oversight.
- Seek mentorship to refine leadership skills and gain insights from experienced professionals.

2. Developing Strong Communication Skills
Leadership requires effective communication. Young professionals should learn to express ideas clearly, listen actively, and provide constructive feedback.

Example:

> *Taylor Morgan*, a new sales associate at Everline Technologies, joined the company's B2B software sales team shortly after graduating from Temple University. In her first few months, Taylor struggled with client objections, especially around pricing and product differentiation in a competitive market.

Rather than becoming discouraged, Taylor took action. She enrolled in a persuasive communication workshop offered by the company's learning and development team, and began studying successful pitches from senior colleagues. She also worked closely with her mentor, *Raj Gupta*, a senior account executive, to refine her messaging and objection-handling techniques.

Taylor revamped her pitch to focus on value-driven storytelling, highlighting how Everline's platform helped clients reduce operational costs and improve workflow efficiency. She practiced role playing scenarios and tailored her presentations to each client's specific pain points.

Employers value employees who proactively develop their communication and leadership skills, positioning themselves as future leaders.

Leading by Example and Inspiring Colleagues
Leaders set positive examples, motivate their teammates, and foster collaboration; employees who demonstrate reliability, enthusiasm, and strong work ethics uplift those around them.

1. Demonstrating a Strong Work Ethic

Leading by example means showing dedication, accountability, and resilience in professional settings.

Example:

> *Maya Thompson*, an entry level operations associate at Silverline Logistics, joined the company fresh out of Rutgers University. While still learning the ropes, Maya quickly became known for her reliability and professionalism. She consistently met deadlines, communicated clearly, and maintained a positive attitude, even during high-pressure periods.
>
> Beyond her assigned tasks, Maya often stepped in to help colleagues troubleshoot issues with inventory tracking software and workflow bottlenecks. She created a simple guide for new team members and offered to lead informal peer training sessions.
>
> Her manager, *Elliot Greene*, noticed that Maya's consistency and collaborative spirit were raising the bar for the entire team. Her peers began emulating her work ethic and approach to problem solving.

Best Practices:

- Stay proactive rather than waiting for instructions.
- Encourage team collaboration and create a supportive work environment.
- Be approachable - offering guidance to colleagues fosters unity and teamwork.

2. Encouraging a Positive Workplace Culture

Young professionals who promote inclusivity, recognize team achievements, and uplift colleagues strengthen workplace morale.

Example:

> *Alexis Monroe*, a project coordinator at SummitEdge Consulting, noticed that her team's morale and engagement was decreasing. Though they worked hard, in the fast-paced environment, her team's contributions often went unnoticed.
>
> To address this, Alexis proposed a team recognition program called *Summit Shoutouts*, designed to celebrate individual and group achievements on a monthly basis. She collaborated with her manager, *David Lin*, and HR partner *Tasha Greene* to design a simple nomination process and a rotating spotlight feature in the company's internal newsletter.
>
> Each month, team members like *Jordan Carlson* (who streamlined a client onboarding process) and *Priya Desai* (who led a successful product launch) were recognized for their contributions. Alexis also organized short shoutout segments during team meetings, where peers could publicly appreciate one another.

Employees who create positive, solution-focused atmospheres inspire success, are invaluable team players.

Strategic Thinking and Decision Making as a Leader
Employers value professionals who assess situations critically, anticipate challenges, and make informed decisions. Strong strategic thinking ensures long term success in leadership roles.

1. Evaluating Challenges and Proposing Solutions

Employees who analyze workplace problems, consider multiple solutions, and make decisions based on logic rather than impulse demonstrate leadership qualities.

Example:

> *Ethan Park*, a business operations associate at Nexora Health Systems, was known for his calm, methodical approach to challenges. When the company began experiencing delays in its internal ticketing system for IT support, frustration grew among employees, but no one had taken the time to investigate the root cause.
>
> Instead of reacting impulsively or placing blame, Ethan took a step back. He gathered data from the past six months of support tickets, interviewed team members like *Lena Ortiz* from HR and *Devon Blake* from Finance, and mapped out the workflow from submission to resolution.
>
> After analyzing the data, Ethan identified two key issues:
>
> 1. A lack of ticket prioritization protocols.
> 2. Redundant approval steps that slowed down resolution times.

He presented three potential solutions to his manager, *Sophie Tran*, each with pros, cons, and implementation timelines. Sophie and the IT team chose a hybrid model that introduced a triage system and automated routing for common requests.

2. Balancing Risk and Opportunity

Great leaders make data driven decisions while weighing risks and benefits carefully. Employers favor candidates who assess challenges from different angles before taking action.

Example:

> *Nina Bajaj*, a junior product manager at Veridian Labs, was leading the development of a new productivity app feature that would allow users to integrate third party calendar tools. While the engineering team was ready to begin development, Nina wasn't convinced the feature would deliver enough value to justify the investment.
>
> Instead of rushing the decision, Nina took a strategic approach. She conducted a market survey targeting current users and gathered feedback through in app polls and user interviews. She also analyzed competitor platforms like TaskNest and FlowSync, noting that while similar features existed, they were underutilized or poorly rated.

To gain a broader perspective, Nina scheduled a meeting with *Elijah Moore*, the company's Director of Product Strategy, and *Samantha Liu*, a senior UX researcher. Together, they reviewed the data and discussed potential alternatives, including a lighter integration that would require fewer resources but still meet user needs.

Professionals who apply strategic thinking contribute significantly to organizational success and innovation.

Final Flex

Employers seek candidates who take initiative, motivate colleagues, and bring effective solutions to the workplace. Young professionals can establish themselves as future leaders by developing leadership skills at any career stage, inspiring teams through action, and practicing strategic decision making.

By embracing these qualities, professionals drive innovation, foster teamwork, and position themselves for long term career success, making them indispensable assets to any organization.

The Final, Final Flex

You've made it to the end of this guide and that's no small feat. If you've read this far, you've already demonstrated one of the most important career competencies: **Intentionality**.

Throughout this journey, we've explored the real-world skills that employers value most, communication, critical thinking, emotional readiness, technology, and leadership. We've unpacked how AI is reshaping the workplace, how your wardrobe can speak volumes, and how your digital brand can open doors before you even knock.

But more than anything, we've focused on **you**. Your **Value**, your **Intent & Credibility**, and your **Confidence**. That's the **VICC framework**, and it's your career compass. It's not just a checklist for job applications; it's a mindset for navigating the professional world with clarity and purpose.

So, here's your final flex:

- **Know your worth.** Employers don't hire resumes; they hire people who understand their unique value and can communicate it with confidence.

- **Lead with intent.** Every email, every interview, every networking moment is a chance to show up with purpose.

- **Build credibility.** Your reputation is your currency. Earn it through consistency, empathy, and excellence.

- **Stay curious.** The future of work is evolving fast. AI, remote collaboration, and digital branding are just the beginning. Keep learning, keep adapting, and keep growing.

This guide isn't the end, it's your launchpad. Use it as a reference, a reminder, and a resource. And remember career readiness isn't about being perfect. It's about being prepared, being intentional, and being unapologetically you.

Now go flex that VICC and build the career that reflects your values, your strengths, and your story.

You've got this. Let me know how it goes!

Self-Assessments

Chapter 2 Self-Assessment: Career Competencies in the Age of AI

Instructions: For each statement below, rate yourself on a scale from 1 to 5:
1 = Strongly Disagree | 2 = Disagree | 3 = Neutral | 4 = Agree | 5 = Strongly Agree

Career Readiness & Core Competencies
1. I can clearly and professionally communicate my ideas in writing and in conversation.
2. I work well in teams and contribute meaningfully to group projects.
3. I can analyze problems and make decisions using logic and evidence.
4. I consistently demonstrate professionalism, reliability, and a strong work ethic.
5. I am comfortable using digital tools relevant to my field of interest.
6. I value and contribute to inclusive environments where diverse perspectives are respected.
7. I take initiative and seek leadership opportunities when possible.
8. I actively pursue opportunities for career and personal development.
Notes:

____

____

____

____

Adaptability & Lifelong Learning

9. I embrace change and adapt quickly to new situations or challenges.

10. I seek feedback and use it to improve my performance.

11. I am open to learning new technologies and tools, even if they are outside my comfort zone.

12. I have a growth mindset and believe my skills can improve with effort and practice.

<u>Notes:</u>

AI Awareness & Future Readiness

13. I understand how AI is impacting my field or industry.

14. I have completed or plan to complete an AI-related credential or course.

15. I can critically evaluate AI-generated content or data.

16. I am aware of ethical considerations related to AI, such as bias and privacy.

17. I believe human-centered skills like empathy, creativity, and judgment will remain essential in the workplace.

18. I am preparing to work alongside AI tools rather than compete with them.

<u>Notes:</u>

____

____

____

____

____

____

Reflection Questions

- Which competencies do you feel strongest in?
- Which areas would you like to improve over the next 6-12 months?
- How can you use internships, mentorships, or alumni connections to strengthen your career readiness?
- What steps can you take to become more AI-literate and future-ready?

<u>Reflection Notes:</u>

____

____

____

____

____

____

Chapter 4: Communication Audit · Self-Assessment Worksheet

Instructions: For each statement below, rate yourself on a scale from 1 to 5:
1 = Strongly Disagree | 2 = Disagree | 3 = Neutral | 4 = Agree | 5 = Strongly Agree

Verbal Communication
1. I speak clearly and confidently in meetings and presentations.
2. I adapt my tone and language based on my audience.
3. I organize my thoughts before speaking.
4. I actively participate in team discussions.
Notes:

____

____
____
____

____

____

Written Communication
5. I write emails and messages that are clear and professional.
6. I tailor my writing style to suit different audiences.
7. I proofread my written communication before sending.
8. I use bullet points and formatting to improve readability.
Nonverbal Communication

9. I maintain good posture and eye contact during conversations.

10. I use facial expressions and gestures to reinforce my message.

11. I am aware of how my body language affects others.

12. I avoid defensive or closed-off nonverbal cues.

Notes:

____

____

____

____

____

____

Digital Communication

13. I present myself professionally in video calls.

14. I follow etiquette when using Slack, Teams, or other messaging platforms.

15. I maintain a consistent and authentic personal brand online.

16. I use LinkedIn or other platforms to share professional content.

Notes:

____

____

____

____

____

____

Reflection Questions
- Which communication areas are your strengths?
- Which areas do you want to improve?
- What steps can you take to enhance your
communication skills?

<u>Reflection Notes:</u>

____
____
____
____
____
____

Action Plan:
- Goal 1:

____
____

- Goal 2:

____
____

- Goal 3:

____
____

Chapter 4: Reframing the Word 'I' - Writing Exercise

Instructions: Below are common self-focused statements often used in cover letters, resumes, or interviews. Example:

Original: I managed the social media accounts for our student organization.
Revised: Managed social media accounts to increase student engagement and promote campus events.
Exercise:
1. Original: I organized a fundraising event for our club.
Revised:

____

____

2. Original: I created a newsletter for alumni outreach.
Revised:

____

____

3. Original: I developed a presentation for our marketing class.
Revised:

____

____

4. Original: I helped new students get oriented during welcome week.

Revised:

____

____

5. Original: I led a team project in my business course.
Revised:

____

____

Reflection Questions
- What did you notice when shifting the focus from 'I' to impact?
- How might this change the way an employer perceives your experience?
- What other statements in your resume or cover letter could be reframed?

<u>Reflection Notes:</u>

____

____

____

____

____

____

Chapter 7: Professional Wardrobe Checklist & Budget Friendly Style Builder

Investing in your wardrobe is investing in yourself. When you look good, you feel good and when you feel good…

Essential Wardrobe Checklist:
· 1-2 Blazers (neutral colors like black, navy, or gray)
· 2-3 Button-down shirts or blouses
· 2-3 Pairs of dress slacks or chinos
· 1-2 Professional dresses or skirts (if applicable)
· 1 Pair of clean, polished dress shoes
· 1 Sweater or cardigan for layering
· 1 Professional bag or briefcase
· Neutral belt and accessories
· Undergarments suitable for professional attire
· Optional: Tie, watch, or subtle jewelry

Budget-Friendly Style Builder Exercise
Step 1: Set Your Budget
Monthly wardrobe budget: $________________________

Step 2: Identify Your Priorities
Which items do you need most right now?

____

____

____

____

Step 3: Explore Affordable Options
· Thrift stores or consignment shops
· Online sales and outlet stores
· Clothing swaps with friends
· Tailoring inexpensive items for better fit

Step 4: Plan Your Purchases
What will you buy this month?

____

____

____

Step 5: Reflect and Reassess
How do you feel when you dress professionally?

____

____

____

What message does your wardrobe send to others?

____

____

____

Style Goal:
By the end of this semester/season, I will build a
wardrobe that helps me:
· Feel confident
· Show up professionally
· Align with my career goals

Signature: _______________________________ Date:________

Chapter 7: Dress for Success/ Weekly Outfit Planner

Plan your wardrobe with intention. When you look good, you feel good and when you feel good, you show up…

Monday
Outfit:

____

____

Meetings/Events:

____

____

Goal/Message:

____

____

Tuesday
Outfit:

____

____

Meetings/Events:

____

____

Goal/Message:

____

____

Wednesday
Outfit:

____

____

Meetings/Events:

____

____

Goal/Message:

____

____

Thursday
Outfit:

____

____

Meetings/Events:

____

____

Goal/Message:

____

____

Friday
Outfit:

____

____

Meetings/Events:

____

____

Goal/Message:

____

____

Reflection Questions
- How did your wardrobe choices support your
confidence and professionalism this week?
- What adjustments will you make next week?

<u>Reflection Notes:</u>

____

____

____

____

____

____

Chapter 12 Self-Assessment: Measuring Digital Fluency

Regular evaluation of digital skills ensures continuous improvement and identifies areas for focused development.

Instructions: For each statement below, rate yourself on a scale from 1 to 5:
1 = Strongly Disagree | 2 = Disagree | 3 = Neutral | 4 = Agree | 5 = Strongly Agree

Tool Proficiency:

I can effectively use digital tools to accomplish professional tasks.

Problem Solving Application:

I can identify opportunities where digital tools can solve workplace challenges.

Learning Agility:

I quickly adapt to and integrate new technologies into existing workflows.

Security Awareness:

I consistently apply cybersecurity best practices in my daily work.

Collaboration Effectiveness:

I work well with others using digital platforms and tools.

<u>Notes:</u>

Professional Recognition Opportunities: Digital fluency achievements provide valuable content for resumes, performance reviews, and professional networking.

Documentation Strategies:

- Create a portfolio of digital projects and process improvements

- Quantify efficiency gains and cost savings from digital tool implementation

- Obtain relevant certifications in cloud platforms, security practices, or data analysis tools

- Share knowledge through blog posts, presentations, or professional organization contributions

- Mentor colleagues in digital skill development

Jerry D. Goldstein is a career readiness leader, mentor, and connector who has helped thousands of students and young professionals launch meaningful careers by opening his network, offering honest guidance, and translating the unspoken expectations of the professional world into skills anyone can learn. Known for his practical, human approach, Jerry has built some of the most active alumni and mentoring communities in higher education and has personally coached emerging professionals across industries, from business and media to technology, nonprofit, and the arts. His work centers on empowerment and access: giving students not just advice, but real opportunities, relationships, and confidence.

For more than a decade, Jerry has been the person students call when they feel stuck, uncertain, or overlooked and the mentor who stays in their corner long after they land the job. *Spilling The Career Tea* brings together the lessons, stories, and frameworks he's shared in thousands of one-on-one conversations, offering a clear roadmap to show up with value, intent, credibility, and confidence from day one.